Oils

from scratch

Oils

from scratch

Art Workshop with Paul

Paul Taggart

Sandcastle
Books

First Published in Great Britain in 2006 by
Sandcastle Books Limited
The Stables
Sheriffs Lench Court
Sheriffs Lench
Nr. Evesham
Worcs. WR11 4SN

www.sandcastlebooks.co.uk

ISBN 0-9552478-1-0

Printed and bound in Thailand

Contents

Oil
PRINCIPLES

Oil paint is a rich and robust medium, whose beauty is reliant on its internal glow and tactile nature. By fully exploiting the characteristics of the paint, whether in its raw buttery form, or thinned down to an oily fluid, artists have at their disposal an extensive range of possibilities. Not surprising that oil painting has been the favoured choice for artists over many centuries.

The principles of oil painting can take you on a journey from the simplest of washy oil sketches through to the rich, lustrous results of a traditional technique in which the paint is built up in layers, from dark to light.

The versatility afforded by this medium in enabling the artist to produce spontaneous paintings, all-in-one-go, or to work over a period of time to achieve a more developed piece, makes oil painting attractive to beginners and professionals alike.

Techniques such as tinting and glazing with transparent mixes of glowing colour, provide the very essence of brilliance and depth associated with paintings in oil; whether they be most highly detailed, or dramatically bold. From the smallest of miniatures painted on gesso, to the larger than life masterpieces on canvas, oil painting is in a world of its own.

The underlying structure of snow-clad forms within a landscape are brought to life by exploiting the inherent textures of an applied surface, thick paint, transparent glazes and bristle brushes – pages 90 to 93.

The principles of Oils from Scratch *will guide you along the way to understanding this exciting medium. From a grounding in the basics of the tools that make up a simple painting kit, you are then taken through the process of working with colour, into your first projects.*

The pages are filled with information, which will require a patient approach. Allow yourself time to take this in from the outset, be prepared to follow the steps at a pace that suits you and the pleasures of working with oils will be realised.

This book is structured around simple exercises that demonstrate the main aspects of a particular set of tools, beginning with paints. Having then similarly covered brushes, palettes and surfaces, the tools are revisited and exploited to produce a series of projects in the form of exercises followed by stage-by-stage paintings.

Slabs of paint applied with a painting knife with which to experience the tactile nature of oil paint on - pages 66 to 69.

Be forgiving with yourself throughout the process

of learning how to paint in oils. Persevere with the

exercises, even if they go wrong, as there is much to

be learnt from making mistakes.

To fully exploit this medium it is important to understand the basics of colour mixing and application. The section dedicated to this subject demonstrates a straightforward, no nonsense approach to the myriad of possibilities at any artists disposal.

A 'jungle' of forms in this woodland scene prove ideal to exploit brush-strokes in the project on pages 74 to 77.

Use the exercises time and again, to gain a better understanding of the tool in use, or the technique being exploited. By working on them in conjunction with the stage-by-stage paintings, not merely in isolation, you will gain much more insight into how each can be best achieved.

So many potential oil painters are frustrated at their first attempts and sadly some not only shy away from working with oils, but give up painting altogether. This is a disappointing turn of events that can be prevented, along with any sense of failure on the part of the would-be painter.

In Oils From Scratch it is my intention to introduce beginners to oil painting in a comfortable manner, one that demystifies what can be perceived as a medium that requires extensive skill to be effective. Whilst it is true to say that working with oil paints at the most advance stage does require skill developed over a period of time, it is nonetheless equally true to say that effective and exciting results can be achieved from the outset of this journey.

Not only is this book intended for beginners, it should prove useful in opening up further possibilities for those who already paint and provide a gateway to other techniques. Finally, nothing would delight me more than to know that my love for this particular medium has helped to bring someone back to painting, through the pages of this book.

Which paints do I need?

Whilst it is possible to work with some types of paint without fully understanding their nature, to do so with oil paints could prove deeply frustrating.

This is a rich and exciting medium and not to fully exploit its potential would be to miss a fulfilling experience. What a pity that would be, especially if all that stands between you and the enjoyment of oil painting is lack of information about the basics.

WHILST ALL PAINTS ARE primarily produced from the same pigments, it is the glue that binds them to the surface which distinguishes them. Over the years a variety of glues have been used in paint mixes, such as soap, wax, raw eggs, gum and oil. Modern binding agents, including acrylic, have more recently been added to the varieties of paint with which an artist can work.

These glues, known as mediums, give a particular paint its characteristics. The medium in oil paints is oil, which makes this a painting medium that is strong and long lasting.

Oil can be kept thick or made more fluid, so it is, therefore, with oil paint. Its versatility enables artists to not only produce structured, heavy brush-strokes, but to also work with a thinned down mixture that flows easily.

Oil paint will stick to most grounds, provided they are not too absorbent or slippery. Preparing a suitable ground is a simple matter of sizing and priming. This has enabled artists to work on a wide variety of grounds, exploiting their individual finish and texture; grounds such as glass, metal, plaster, ivory, wood, paper and canvas.

These inherent qualities naturally affect the characteristic marks the paint will make as it is applied, for it easily responds to the nature of the surface over which it is laid. On smooth surfaces it is capable of fine detail and miniature paintings of incredible delicacy are possible. Across heavy canvas, bolder brushwork is demanded, such as the juicy strokes in the work of the Impressionists.

Each artist finds his or her own way to exploit the paint. The palette knife painter will use paint directly from the tube, in which the pigment is mixed with just the right amount of medium to give it a buttery consistency. Because the paint does not shrink as it dries, the resultant finish will remain perfect and intact as it does so, whatever depth of paint is applied, or surface textured created.

Others prefer to use the paint more fluidly. It is possible to float fluid colour across a surface and while the layer is still wet, brush and work further paint into it. This produces a vigorous and exciting result where the colours meld on the painting surface itself. Many artists have invented their own secret mediums for such a purpose. Using the right blends of specific oils and thinners, they concocted a medium that possessed the viscosity and drying time that suited their particular technique.

Past artists not only had the task of creating their own mediums, but they also had to find and produce their own pigments. This could prove restrictive, for more often than not they had to work with the raw materials that were to hand or readily available. The abundance of earth colours naturally gave birth to their popularity. However, bright pigments were much more of a rarity. Furthermore the available pigments might not have been very permanent.

Today's artist is spoilt for choice. Pigments are available from all corners of the globe. Dyes can be created chemically, to produce colours that would once have been unheard of. This in some ways causes a dilemma, for there is so much choice.

When starting out in oil painting it is better to concentrate on working with a few materials and understanding how to exploit these to the fullest. By beginning with the basics, fully understanding the nature of oil paint and how it can be made to work in different ways, you will be helped on your way to gaining the confidence required to move on to the next stage.

Play with the paint in the first instance, get used to its feel. While experimenting you can be relaxed about the results, which is vitally important if you are to enjoy what oil painting has to offer.

Understanding paints

Basic Constituents and Painting Process

BASIC CONSTITUENTS - Oil paint is composed of two main elements. Dry pigment (powdered colour)...

...and a glue (medium), which fixes the paint to the surface. Linseed oil is the traditional medium.

Within the tube, the mix of ground pigment and medium is balanced to produce a thick, easily textured paint.

The consistency of the oil paint can be adjusted by adding a thinner or more medium.

PAINTING PROCESS - FIRST LAYER (UNDERPAINTING) - Thinner is added to tube consistency paint. This spreads out both pigment and oil and accelerates drying.

SECOND LAYER (IMPASTO) - Thick textured paint is applied without addition of any thinners or medium.

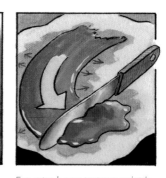

For extra heavy textures paint is made less fluid by spreading out on absorbent paper. This soaks up oil from the paint, leaving it drier and stiffer.

When sufficient oil has been removed, paint is scraped off paper and returned to palette, ready for use.

The object of the second layer is to create the structure of the painting, from dark to light values, through the gradual build up of stiff paint.

This second layer is left to become surface dry - the skin of the paint must not be broken or it will expose the wet paint beneath.

Basic Constituents and Painting Process

THIRD LAYER (GLAZING) - Glazing brings an oil painting to life; it enriches the colours and enhances textures. A glaze comprises of glazing medium...

ARTSTRIPS©

...to which a small amount of colour is added. The result is a transparent colour mix.

Painted over the previously built up impasto layer, glazes will run into its textures, to enhance the quality of each brush-stroke.

Glazes can be painted lightly over the whole painting - to hold the colours together, or alternatively...

...over specific areas and/or blended into other glazes on the surface.

THIRD LAYER (TINTING) . The addition of white to a glaze produces a tint. Zinc white is preferable as it is the most transparent.

Worked into the surface, like a glaze, a tint adds depth and atmosphere.

TIP [AT ANY STAGE - WHEN SURFACE IS DRY] - OILING OUT - Retouching varnish is applied to prevent uneven shine and protect pigment.

Understanding paints
Basic constituents and qualities

The colour in paint (known as pigment), can be acquired in powder form. These pigments are obtained from many sources and from different parts of the world. Genuine Artists' Quality paints vary considerably in price from colour to colour. The makers give the paints a series or group number, which denotes the price. This price does not signal quality differences between individual colours, it reflects the cost of producing them, particularly the cost of the pigment used.

Earth colours are therefore relatively cheap, whilst at the other end of the scale, genuine Ultramarine, whose pigment is obtained from ground Lapis Lazuli (a semi-precious stone) can be costly.

Tubes sold as 'oil paint for artists' are usually cheaper, student varieties, generally packaged and marketed under a different brand/range name. In these the colour is often a chemical dye, created to match the genuine pigment. Thus all the colours in the range can be kept at the same price. Students' Quality paints may not be as well ground, or have the same colour saturation as the Artists' Quality. However, they usually handle with sufficient distinction for a beginner to experience the full richness of oil painting.

Permanency is the term used to denote the lightfast properties of any one paint, when exposed to daylight and its durability, when exposed to normal degrees of atmospheric pollution. The price of a colour is no guarantee of its permanency. In point of fact, the 'manufactured', cheaper Students' Quality paints are likely to feature a more evenly distributed permanency rating across the range. Artists' Quality paints, on the other hand, can vary considerably, depending on the source from which their pigment is obtained.

Tubes are usually marked with star rating or letters, to indicate permanency. It is sensible to check the degree rating of any particular brand against the relevant colour chart, which will detail that brands rating system.

NOTE - THE GROUP/SERIES NUMBER THAT APPEARS ON THE TUBE IS NOT THE DEGREE RATING. IT MERELY INDICATES THE PRICE CATEGORY IN WHICH THE COLOUR FALLS.

Many manufacturers produce colour charts featuring the actual paint (as opposed to a printed equivalent) - these more accurately show the hue, strength and transparency of a colour. It is worth consulting this, for it could save expensive mistakes being made.

Some form of glue is required to apply and fix the powdered pigment to the surface. The basis of any paint is this glue, known as the medium. In oil painting this is an oil, which dries hard to create a permanent, coloured layer. The traditional medium is refined linseed oil, but others are also used. Refined safflower oil for example, which is often used in whites to ensure purity of colour and resistance to yellowing.

Basic types

In any tube of oil paint the main constituents fall into three categories – [1] Pigment/Colour (red section) [2] Extending agent or filler pigment (grey section) [3] Medium (gold section). Some pigments are so powerful that filler pigments are needed to prevent the colour from overwhelming colour mixes on the palette. Unfortunately however, the greater the quantity of filler, the weaker the colour becomes.

Cheap paints contain more filler and although these may still look good in the tube, the colour will be less effective once mixed with other colours.

Paint containing lots of pigment is saturated with colour and while it does cost more, will yield the best results.

All these constituents are ground together. The traditional method for hand grinding is pestle and mortar, while in large scale manufacturing the mix is ground between rollers. Once thoroughly ground, the resultant paint is sealed in tubes to prevent the oil within from reacting chemically with the air, which would otherwise make it harden.

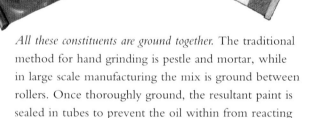

Basic nature

The amount of medium added to the pigment in oil paint is carefully balanced so as to yield a stiff mixture, when used straight from the tube. This is ideal for creating surface texture, known as impasto – the hallmark of the oil painting technique.

White paints

Whites are essential for building texture in an oil painting and for adding light.

Foundation White – used for priming previously sized surfaces. Can be dissolved into a thin layer with the addition of turpentine.

Underpainting White – can be used throughout the painting process. It mixes well with colours. It is also stable and dries to a matt finish. Fast drying, it builds impasto layers with ease.

Painting Whites – these can crack if layered thickly and over painted before thoroughly dry: –

• *Titanium (Permanent) White* – the most popular. An opaque and versatile white.

• *Zinc White* – the most transparent white. An absolute essential for tinting.

• *Flake White* – fast drying, but lacks the opacity of Titanium White or the whiteness of Zinc white.

Mediums for oil paint

In oil painting, the surface becomes more and more exciting as layers of colour are built up over one another. To ensure that these are stable and not liable to cracking, it is prudent to layer the paint 'lean to fat'. A traditional technique, in which the painting is created layer upon layer, in order that it dries progressively and evenly, so that the layers shrink at the same rate and do not split.

A 'fat' layer is one where additional oil is mixed into the paint, which therefore dries more slowly. Consequently it must be near the surface of the painting so that the air can reach it first. Transparent glazes for the final layer are created with the addition of an oily (fat) medium.

For a 'lean' layer, the binding oil already present in tube colours is thinned down with a thinner, such as Artists' Distilled Turpentine.

The stiff paint in the tube has a balanced amount of oil - just enough to make it buttery in consistency.

Many mediums mix well with the pigment and may be preferred for faster or slower drying rates, or even because they produce a more flexible film when dry. However, oils on their own tend to be a little brittle when dry and thinner is therefore added to reduce this tendency. The resultant mix is known as a 'glazing medium'.

Alkyd mediums are intermixable with oil paint and are both faster drying and more flexible when dry. Often brown in colour, the colour dissipates when mixed so that it does not affect the colour. As well as the more fluid consistency variety in bottles, gels of different viscosity (stiffness) are available in tubes.

GLAZING - colour thinned to transparency with the addition of a glazing medium. Its component colour will intensify, enrich, or dull the colour it covers. As this thin mixture runs into the dry, previously painted oil textures, these qualities are enhanced or strengthened. Inevitably a glaze will darken the colour over which it is laid.

TINTING - a coloured glaze with white added, whose opacity level is controlled by the amount of white added. A tint will lighten, dull or soften the area over which it is applied.

Exercise for paints

The application of final detail need not be limited to use of a Rigger brush. As long as the colour mix has enough glazing medium to allow it to flow easily, a soft round brush will prove equally effective, providing that it points well. Although a bristle is not inappropriate for the job, it will tend to yield a broader, scuffed line, which may be suitable for certain subjects.

Once applied, the line-work, being a colour mix with medium added, will stay wet long enough to be blended. This blending is better tackled with a soft round brush and can be carried out at the end of a line, or used to soften one side of the line, effectively turning the blended side into an edge.

Towards the end of a painting you may feel the need for a little detail, or drawing, to add focus and finish off. Fine line-work and accents are easily applied at this stage, by making the paint fluid once again, with the addition of a glazing medium.

For this exercise the impasto layer of paint is kept very light in value. The gentle pink and green brush-strokes, used for the petals and leaves, follow the direction of growth. This provides an underlying rhythm and structure over which a web of line-work is drawn.

A nylon Rigger brush proves ideal for this job and different colour mixes are used to depict leaf or petal. Note that white is also used for some of the line-work, to support the darker rhythms and provide a line highlight.

Why do I need a bristle brush?

Oil paint is unlike any other medium and needs something very special with which it can be successfully transferred to the painting surface. What is required is a brush that will respond to the inherent nature of oil paint, allowing the artist to exploit its full potential.

WHEN INTRODUCED TO OIL PAINTING BRUSHES for the first time, most would-be painters find them ungainly. How is it possible to achieve results from a brush that is so long, awkward and stiff? It takes a little while to realise that, as with any superb tool, it is exactly fitted to the job.

How exactly does the oil painting brush respond to the qualities of oil paint?

As always the best way in which to discover this is by putting one to work. This section will point you in the right direction and there is nothing to compare with getting the feel and balance of these brushes between your fingers. You will soon discover that there are a plethora of different shapes and sizes of brush to choose from. Where do you start? Which do you pick?

The answer lies in the paint itself. The paint in a tube has been perfectly mixed to give the correct balance between colour content and stiffness of character. To apply this directly to the painting surface requires a brush with strong stiff filaments in its head.

Not only must this brush hold and master the paint, but it must be flexible enough to deposit the colour fluidly. It will also face the rigours of brushing paint over surfaces that have often dried to the consistency of rough sandpaper, without shredding in the first few strokes. This is a lot to ask of a brush and it is not surprising that the traditional oil painting bristle brush looks so intimidating at first glance.

Paint is not always applied at tube consistency; it can be let down and made more fluid with the addition of thinners and mediums. Although the bristle brush can be used with more fluid paint, it is not really designed to do so.

Take glazing, as an example, where the fluid colours need to flow across the surface in a succulent wash. Glazes run into and discover irregularities in the surface, allowing us to see the structure of the surface paint strokes. In glazing it is the colour mix that reveals the textures, not the brush with which it is applied.

TIPS:

• Always clean brushes at the end of a painting session.

• When drying a brush out, stand it in a jar, never on its head.

• Brushes made of natural hair must be protected against moth attack.

On the other hand, the bristle brush is designed to create its own textures. The stiff bristles in the head will create grooves or rivulets in the surface of any paint layer that it is being used to apply. If used for glazing, the resultant texture would tend to obscure the underlying structure, resulting in a confused and dirty finish. Whilst this problem could be overcome to some degree, by working the glaze into the impasto beneath, it is more practical to have a brush best suited for glazing.

A range of soft-haired brushes would fit the bill, their strength being the ability to lay a smooth, even surface of fluid paint. When soft-haired brushes are used to apply the fluid mix over a smooth surface, the applied colour remains smooth. When applied over dry impasto paint however, the fluid colour runs into and exposes the structure beneath, rather than creating its own texture.

In effect therefore, specific brushes are required to perform a particular function within any one layer in an oil painting.

Soft brushes are available in a multitude of varieties. The most important element being the difference in the type of filament from which the head is made. Natural hair brushes are generally considered the most responsive to detail. Since each hair naturally tapers to a point, the collective head offers a marvellous point.

Natural hairs also possess a flexible bounce, which allows better control and shaping during use. Admittedly, whilst Sable haired brushes are best of all, the cheaper Ox and Squirrel hair alternatives work well, but are softer in nature.

Whilst natural hair is superb in use, it is not particularly hard wearing, especially when dragged across any rough surface textures. This is where nylon brushes offer the ideal option. Not only do they mimic many of the qualities required, they are also stronger and generally less expensive. When they ultimately wear down, as all oil painting brushes do, it is not quite so costly to replace them.

Furthermore, nylon possesses one other excellent quality - it does not absorb water. Why should this be important in oil painting? At the end of each painting session, oil painting brushes need to be cleaned well in soap and water. Bristle brushes will absorb water if left in contact with any water for too long a period. When the bristles swell they splay out from the base of the brush head and the head loses its shape. Artists now have a choice of nylon brushes that not only mimic the soft natural hair brushes, but also the traditional stiff bristle oil painting brush.

Along with the round shapes, oil painting brushes come in a wide variety of shapes and lengths. It is always sensible to choose those with as long a head as possible for two reasons.

First, a long head means flexibility and thus more efficient paint application. Second, as oil painting brushes do wear down, the longer the head, the longer it will be of use.

COMMON TERMS

In this book I have standardised the terms applied to the use of brushes, in order to make things simpler for those new to painting.

The handle of a brush is known as the shaft. Traditionally made of wood with a sturdy coating, but plastic and other materials are also used these days.

The hairs, or filaments, that make up the brush head are set into a ferrule, the collar that holds the brush head to the shaft. The hairs are most likely to be set into the ferrule with glue, which can soften when warmed. Generally this ferrule is made from metal, although in some specialist brushes other materials are used. Always wash brushes in cold or very tepid water, to prevent the metal ferrule from expanding and the glue softening, which would result in hairs falling out of the brush head.

Understanding brushes

Round brush - nature

ROUND BRISTLE - the most versatile. The head should be as long as possible so that it can flex to deliver paint.

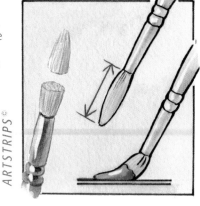

SOFT ROUND - made from natural hair. Has a fine point for detail.

Round brushes with nylon filaments are available and mimic the nature of both bristle and natural hair.

Round brush - usage

ROUND BRISTLE - the stiff hairs create surface texture when used with stiff oil paint.

SOFT ROUND - creates smooth layer of paint.

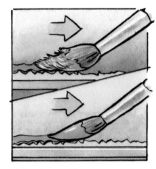

All brushes suffer damage when pulled across a dry oil-painted surface. Nylon is tougher and cheaper than the natural hair equivalents.

Generations of artists have used brushes with round heads, so they have easily proved their worth over the centuries. The secret of a round brush is the fact that it can be rotated whilst painting on the surface, as a brush-stroke is being applied.

Although this does take practice, it provides the artist with a stroke that can travel much further. Paint is deposited from the full circumference of the brush head, rather than merely from one face. Similarly, a greater number of smaller strokes can be applied between paint loading.

Rotating the brush also tends to deposit deeper paint on the side of the brush-stroke toward which the brush is turned. This banking up of paint can prove very useful in reinforcing an edge.

These techniques rely on using the brush shoulder. However, a soft round brush has the added benefit of a point that is excellent for carrying out detail work. Many new to painting assume that a very small brush is required to produce detail. The fact is if the right brush is chosen, a larger size will produce an equally fine point, with the added benefit of being able to hold more colour in its head – ideal for continuous working.

Other brushes

FLAT BRISTLE - excellent for scumbling and creating sharp-edged brush-strokes.

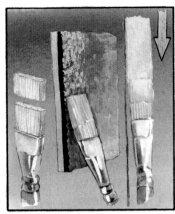

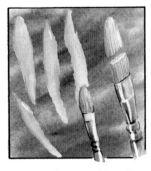

FILBERT - shares qualities with the other brushes and creates softer, more rounded brush-strokes.

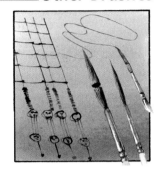

RIGGER - made for fluid line-work. Paint must be thinned with thinner or medium, to produce lines.

Brush cleaning

Remove excess colour on a tissue. Gently squeeze and roll - never pull.

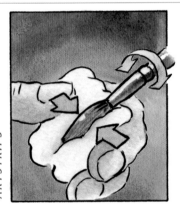

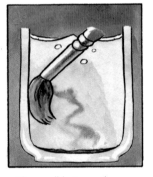

Rinse well in turpentine substitute or white spirit. Press gently against side of jar and rotate to remove paint from inside brush head.

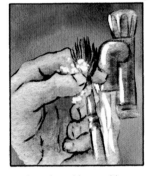

Wash under cold or tepid water (never hot) with soap. Gently massage head to remove colour from inside. Repeat until all colour is removed.

With the round brush as the main stay of the painting kit, others can be included to perform specialist functions. Flat brushes are almost as popular as rounds. They do create a brushy surface, which suits the nature of oil painting. Since flat brushes cannot be rotated during usage, they need to be replenished with paint more frequently. This makes them less appropriate for wet-in-wet painting. The main strength of the flat brush comes to the fore when working over dry paint, where it can skate across the surface, working from and up to, any sharp edges of the subject.

For fluid line and drawing there is nothing to equal the Rigger brush. But the value of a Rigger does not stop there, for it can be pushed and dragged on the surface so that the head opens up to produce unexpected strokes. Furthermore, the Rigger can be dipped into juicy deposits of stiffer colour mixes on the palette, which are then dripped or splashed onto the painting. Given the usage that a Rigger brush will be put to in oil painting, it is better to opt for the nylon variety, rather than Sable. Not only is nylon stronger, it also shapes better and has more bounce when used with the heavier oil paint.

SIZING
As sizes vary across all manufacturers, it is not feasible to quote specifics. Whatever size you think you will need, always go for one two sizes larger, as smaller sizes seldom hold enough paint.

Brushes in practice
Round bristle brush: Stiff colour

A generous quantity of stiff, tube consistency paint is required for this study in which to experience the flexibility of the round bristle brush. Mix a dark grey blue, then load a medium sized brush by rotating it in the paint so that every facet of the brush shoulders are covered. To guarantee a healthy supply of paint to the surface, turn the brush as you paint (branches and trunk), or between strokes (leaves and grass). Follow the rhythms of the trunk and leaves, switching the direction of the brush-strokes as you go.

Round nylon brush: Fluid colour

Use both the shoulders of a medium sized brush and the point (for detail). Line-work can also be achieved by flattening the head of the brush on the palette, to form an edge with which to work. The paint needs to be very fluid, by adding fluid alkyd medium and a little thinner to the colour mix. Note how this fluid colour works in a manner not unlike glazing, in that it discovers and reveals the surface texture – in this instance the canvas weave.

Flat bristle brush: Stiff colour

As the flat brush cannot be rotated during loading or application it holds less paint, the brush therefore needs to be loaded more frequently. Use the brush in sideways sweeps (leaves) or pull it in the direction of the shaft to produce short textured strokes (grass). The edge of the brush head can be used for line-work (branches and trunk). Note however, that the edge of the flat brush is a little clumsier to use, than working with the flattened edge of the round brush.

Large Rigger brush: Fluid colour

Working with the Rigger demands quite a fluid mix of colour, with generous quantities of medium and thinner added. Although the Rigger brush is primarily designed to produce line-work (branches and grass), a large Rigger can be swept sideways. This opens up the filaments of the head and, providing the paint is flowing, will deposit irregular strokes of colour wash (leaves). Smaller Riggers could be used to provide finer detail where necessary.

Exercise for brushes

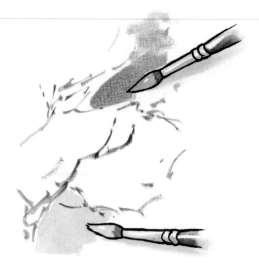

Round bristle brush: Fluid colour Produce a fluid green and a fluid light brown mix on the palette by adding thinner. Use the point of a medium round bristle brush for drawing in the main shapes of the study with these two mixes.

Round nylon brush: Fluid colour Use the shoulder of a round nylon brush to apply fat strokes of fluid colour. The blue colour mix requires generous amounts of alkyd medium and a little thinner. Work down from the top using the transparent colour mix, eventually adding Titanium white to the mix for the lower part of the sky, thus turning it into a semi-opaque tint. Note how the transparent mix brings out the underlying texture of the canvas weave. The opaque tint does this to a much lesser degree.

Flat bristle brush: Stiff colour Colour mixes comprise of stiff, tube consistency paint. Switch to a flat bristle brush to build up the layers of dark to light throughout the greens of the tree and grass. Ease the pressure off the brush and adjust the angle at which you hold it against the surface as the paint layers thicken. Reload the brush frequently as you build the layers, to ensure that the final brush-strokes are well defined and powerful.

Large Rigger brush: Fluid and stiff colour The Rigger brush is superb at producing line-work, when used with a fluid colour mix of paint to which a liberal quantity of medium has been added. Use a dark colour mix to tighten up the exercise with drawing and detail (accents) in fine branches and grasses. Finish off by dripping stiff colour onto the highlights. In this instance therefore, the Rigger brush is used to complete not only the accents, but also the highlights.

This simple exercise will enable you to not only employ a variety of brushes, but will give you the first chance to try painting with different consistencies of colour mix. The study is painted in layers, from dark to lights.

Two important aspects to note as you complete this exercise. First, the amount of dark colour in the final piece. It is so easy to get excited by the lighter colours as they are applied that you can swiftly overdo them. Be prudent; periodically take a break and stand back to assess the overall balance of light against dark.

Second, when applying the lighter strokes you will naturally find that you are developing a rhythm. Unfortunately, this rhythm tends to dominate and strokes become repetitive and regularly spaced. We all suffer from this and you need to take steps to break the pattern. Slow down towards the highlights and place them sparingly and thoughtfully.

Note the irregularity at which the lighter strokes are applied in this study.

Why do I need a palette?

To understand the oil painter's palette fully is to appreciate just how serious and significant a piece of equipment it actually is.

This tool is not merely a piece of wood, its balance and shape can affect your painting experience. Furthermore and most important of all, a correctly laid out and properly used palette will enhance your painting practice.

As a critical factor in exploiting your paints and making the most of colour mixes, it will become one of the most reliable items in your painting kit.

WHENEVER WE VISUALISE the personification of a serious artist we tend to envisage the painter holding a large palette over one arm, clutching a sheaf of long brushes protruding through the finger hold. This image can prove daunting to someone taking up oil painting as a complete beginner, for it may feel somewhat pretentious to be holding and using a palette in the same manner as a professional.

The first question that usually springs to mind is, would an old plate not be sufficient for the job? The answer is simple, it could be, but with some reservations. Whilst the non-absorbent surface of an old plate is adequate, everything else is against it, from its colour, to its shape and weight.

For many of my early painting years, particularly when a student, I used the old metal top from a refrigerator as a palette. It worked very well, being large and perfectly flat. Because the metal was enamelled it did not have any adverse reaction with the paint. However, this makeshift palette would certainly have been more than a little difficult to balance on the forearm and my priority was to avail myself of a decent, traditional wooden palette as soon as I could.

A GOOD PALETTE IS MADE FOR THE JOB

The oil painter's palette should be perfectly flat for easy mixing. It needs to be lightweight, balanced and shaped for comfort. It must be strong enough to withstand the rigours of mixing with knife and brush, to endure vigorous cleaning, and survive the application of solvents and oils to mixes produced on its surface.

The curved shape of the traditional oil palette is specifically designed to fit into the side of the artist's body, as he, or she, stands to paint. Carefully balanced to ease the strain on the supporting arm and wrist, it helps to alleviate the artist from tiring out during a painting session.

Not only are many different types and shapes available, oil palettes are produced in a variety of materials, the top of the range being wood. While the best are relatively expensive, these better quality palettes will last a lifetime if cared for properly.

As well as being ergonomically shaped and balanced, wooden palettes are varnished and/or oiled to prevent excessive absorption of oil from the paints.

Wooden palettes undoubtedly improve with age and usage. Any wood grain initially inherent in the surface, will soon infill with dried paint. Provided the surface is well cleaned at the end of each painting session, over time this surface will become glossy and smooth, to produce an ideal mixing surface. Since it also takes on a darker hue, colours are easier to see against this background and their values more accurately judged.

TIP:

A well cared for palette makes a good palette great
Many palettes are ruined by allowing paint to dry within the mixing areas. Once this occurs the surface becomes more and more textured. Physically, paint becomes lodged in the furrows of the texture as you attempt to mix fresh colour and much is lost. Glazes particularly cannot be seen and judged against such a backdrop of intermingled dry colour. It is essential therefore that cleaning the mixing area on a regular basis should become second nature.

Eventually, the surface becomes so unique that you will take as much pleasure in it as you would the perfectly polished surface of a fine piece of wood furniture. My own palette, a lifelong friend that I pick up every time I work on an oil painting, is burnished to perfection and has caught the eye of more than one of my visiting collectors. It is not however for sale; no matter that it is a sculptural piece in its own right!

SIZE MATTERS
Size really does matter when selecting your main palette. Pick one that is too small and it will undoubtedly prove troublesome.

By the time you have squeezed out all the colours needed, there will be little space left for mixing. Reduce the amount of paint to compensate and you will be constantly unscrewing caps on tubes of paint to renew the colour. Valuable time is not only lost, but your concentration is broken and you will become increasingly frustrated.

Furthermore, if you do not have a good supply of paint on your palette, you will tend to be meagre in its application on the painting. Without plentiful paint, the wet-on-wet layering of colour is impossible to achieve and you will fail to produce the impasto textures that are such an important element in oil painting.

Be organised in the use of your palette, the layout of the colours is of absolute importance, as it is imperative to find a colour without hesitation and know exactly how it will effect a mix to achieve successful results.

There is much advice in the following pages and in the colour mixing section on the best possible arrangement and method.

Understanding palettes

Oil painting palettes can be made from different materials - [top down] mahogany veneer, birch plywood, melamine faced, plastic, glass.

ARTSTRIPS©

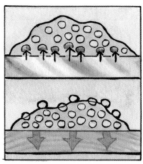

The surface must be non-metallic and non-porous. Metal reacts with pigment and porous surfaces absorb oil, making colours stiff, dull and weak.

Paper palettes, in pad form, are useful for working out of doors. Sheets can be set aside for disposal, or specific mixes kept.

Paint is deposited around outside edge in order that matches position of colours on colour circle - can be left here until it dries, without damaging the surface.

ARTSTRIPS©

Deposit generous amounts of paint around palette. Even soiled brush is less likely to pollute colour when it is not able to touch hard palette surface.

Scrape off paint at palette edge when dry and unusable. Residue is difficult to remove, so simply squeeze fresh paint on top.

Alkyd compatible palette – Alkyd mediums in colour mixes dry much more swiftly than oil. Since these are often present on the palette surface as thin layers of glaze, they dry even faster. During glazing, when the palette may be covered in such glazes, great care needs to be taken that they do not begin to dry out, especially along their edges.

It may therefore be worth having a separate palette for glazing, a surface that is less vulnerable should it need to be scraped – melamine or glass will prove ideal. A smaller palette would be suitable, since only small amounts of colour mix are required for glazing. If the mixing area becomes quickly covered, this will necessitate more frequent cleaning, which in turn reduces the likelihood of mixes drying out.

Palette usage

Paint mixes are created in the centre of the palette, but should never be allowed to dry there.

ARTSTRIPS ©

Remove unwanted mixes with a palette knife. Wipe surface clean and polish with residual oil from paint.

Palette should be held under-hand - provides stable surface required to cope with pressure exerted when mixing.

Palette usage

In this manner the palette is comfortably supported by the arm. Paint deposits are arranged around edge away from the body.

ARTSTRIPS ©

Brushes held under thumb are conveniently accessible, as is cleaning cloth held in fingers.

Finally, large quantity of white laid at one end of palette, with colours additional to the basic six laid at the other.

Clearing up – Every bit of the painting process is hugely enjoyable, with perhaps one exception – the moment when you have to clear up your equipment and clean brushes and surfaces. It is always tempting to leave things and tell yourself that you will clean up later on or tomorrow. Painting can be tiring, the concentration required sees to that and no more so than when working out of doors.

Nevertheless, cleaning is one of the most essential tasks that need to be undertaken. After all, your valuable equipment deserves to be well cared for and replacements will prove costly. That little extra time put into cleaning brushes and palette will pay dividends in the long run, none more so than when it comes to starting the next painting session.

Were brushes and palette to become clogged with paint you simply will not feel like using them and even if you were to do so, they will not do the job properly, no matter how skilled an artist you are.

> **TIP**:
> Always build in fifteen minutes at the end of your painting session schedule to allow for unhurried cleaning of your equipment.

Palettes in practice

Dippers

Dippers are temporary reservoirs for painting mediums and thinners, which clip onto the side of the palette for easy access during painting, or stored away for transport. Transferring mediums and thinners from their original containers prevents the main supply from drying out – which would happen if they were constantly being opened during a painting session.

Available in metal or plastic, the metal variety generally feature brass lids that do not rust. Although dippers without lids are available, the lidded versions are preferable for storage. The airtight lids not only keep air from reaching the contents, to prevent drying out of the medium, but also allow for easy transportation.

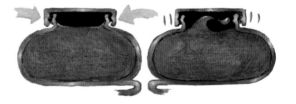

Dippers should be generously filled.
A brush soiled with paint is less likely to deposit its colour when dipped into the medium, providing the brush does not touch the bottom or side of the dipper.

If the content of the dippers starts to thicken, it is best not to add thinners to resin mediums (alkyds) as these will actually dry out faster, even with the lid on. Better to thin alkyds on the surface of the palette. On the other hand, oils will not suffer through being thinned down, in the dipper, with thinners.

NOTE - Always fill dippers at the end of a painting session and ensure lids are screwed tightly to prevent air coming into contact with the contents.

If a medium does develop a skin through drying out – gently cut around the dried 'lid' of medium using a blunt knife, such as a palette knife. Carefully remove this 'lid' and scrape back fluid medium clinging beneath. Refill the dipper to the top with fresh medium.

TIP:

Do not discard miniature glass jars with lids (those used for individual servings of jams etc.) as these make excellent free-standing dippers

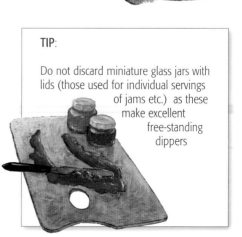

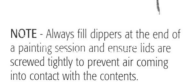

Good palette practice

Get into the habit of generously loading the palette, as there is nothing worse than interrupting your painting flow to search for a tube of colour. Bristle brushes hold a surprising amount of paint inside their heads and before you know it, the paint on the palette has been used up. Should there be insufficient paint on the palette and in the brushes, the technique of layering wet-into-wet is impossible to carry out.

Although none of us like to waste paint, being parsimonious with quantities put on the palette does not ultimately make for good painting practice. Whilst leaving a loaded palette between painting sessions can lead to some of the colours developing a skin, this does not mean that the paint is totally lost. In fact, the skin has protected the paint beneath from being reached by the air, so it remains usable. Whereas paint applied to canvas is not only dried from above, but also from underneath (as air passes through the back of the material) – when on the hard surface of a palette it cannot dry from underneath.

To access the soft colour, simply cut into the mound of paint with a palette knife, peel back and remove the dried skin. Avoid getting any dried skin into paint mixes, as it can prove to be an irritation.

Should any of the paint mixes left over at the end of a painting session be considered useful for further sessions, these can be stored. Scrape the relevant mix into a mound and either move it to the edge of the palette for short-term storage, or onto a separate surface, such as an old plate - cover mix and plate with stretchable food wrap. Alternatively place it in a small jar with airtight lid - or in an open jar filled with water, which will keep the paint wet for some time.

On the other hand, unused paint mixes could be put to use in preparing a ground. Paint mixes are scraped off and applied to a base, such as a prepared canvas, or canvas board, where they build up into areas of interwoven colour and texture. Once completely covered, the prepared ground is left for quite a while until is has dried hard. Sharp edges of paint need to be sanded gently. The result is not only irregular, but means you will also be painting colour on colour - an exciting way in which to start off a painting.

Exercise for palettes

These three cross-sections show how the layers of paint work with one another on the painting surface and how they are created as mixes on the palette surface.

Underpainting Initially the paint is mixed with thinner (either Artists' Distilled turpentine or an odourless thinner), which spreads both the pigment (colour) and the medium (oil) into a thin, transparent layer. To work into the wet surface the thinned paint must be applied with progressively more paint in the mix. Since the wash of colour is so thin, it tends toward transparency, allowing the ground to show through. Brushes used for this stage should all be flexible, so as to lay the colours more readily. The thinner in the mix rapidly evaporates, leaving a thin layer which dries quickly. However, because the oil has been spread thin, this layer is not very strong and can be disturbed by any subsequent vigorous brushwork, even when dry. Retouching varnish, applied as soon as the surface is dry, will protect it.

Impasto layer This layer is rendered with tube consistency paint, in which the colour mixes have no additives of any kind. As the paint remains stiff, it is easily built up into textures, especially when applied with a stiff bristle brush. Several layers can be applied over each other, working from dark to light. Blending of one colour into another is best carried out with a soft nylon round brush. Paint mixes on the palette should be mixed with a stiff bristle brush, which creates streaky, exciting results. Depending on the depth of the layers and the colours used, this stage can take some time to dry. Should glazing be considered for the next stage in a painting, as in this exercise, colours will benefit from being a little light, through the addition of white - even though they will tend to appear slightly chalky. This layer must be left to dry thoroughly before moving on to the next stage of glazing and/or tinting.

Glazing The third layer in this exercise comprises of glazing i.e. colour mixed with glazing medium. In effect, this means adding more oil to the colour, creating a transparent fluid layer that discovers the nooks and crannies of the previously laid impasto. Colours therefore become darker and richer and their texture is enhanced. Whilst colours can be mixed on the palette with either bristle or nylon brushes, they should be applied to the surface with a soft brush. As the glaze layers build up, the painting now darkens gradually and the colours intensify.

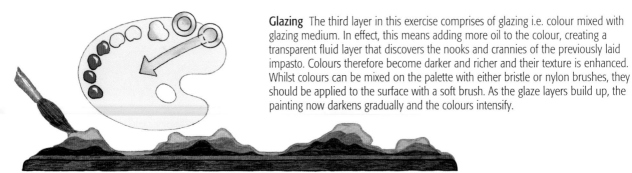

This study describes the regular palette mixes used during the layering of oil paint, an approach known as working 'Lean to Fat'.

In reality the layers would be built on top of each other across the whole of the painting surface; here however, the layers are demonstrated separately so that they can be more easily examined and understood.

LEAN LAYER - [visible in the red area] - a layer of thinned colours applied across the whole of the painting surface. A Rigger brush was used to produce the drawing into this layer, using thinned mixes of dark colour with a slightly thicker consistency.

IMPASTO LAYER - [visible in the blue area] - the lean layer has been over painted using tube consistency paint. This layer is built up from darks rubbed into the surface with a bristle brush through to the highlights dripped on with a Rigger brush.

FAT LAYER - [restricted to the yellow area] - once the impasto layer dried, this area was finished off with glazes through the addition of oil to paint mixes, hence the term 'fat'. These transparent colours excite both the colour and texture of the impasto layer over which they are applied.

Why do I need a special surface on which to paint in oils?

The answer is simple - Oil paint will soak down into any base that has not been properly prepared, which means it will not flow on the painting surface, nor can it be blended. Thus the painting becomes dull and dismal almost immediately and the most important characteristics of oil paint have been lost from the start.

THE PROBLEM DOES NOT STOP THERE.

Migration of oil from the paint through the ground is also destructive to both. The paint, deprived of oil, becomes dull and lacklustre. Since the oil is the glue that holds the pigment to the surface, the paint layer has become vulnerable.

Varnishing will not help, because varnish soaking into the exposed pigment now acts as the binder. This is fine, until you need to remove the varnish for cleaning and restoring purposes. As the varnish is removed the colour will come away with it.

The ground also suffers. Soaked with oil, it can now begin to discolour and disintegrate.

The solution to these problems is a simple one - place a barrier between the paint and the ground, one that will hold the paint securely, but not allow the oil to seep through. This is why the base on which you will be working must be properly prepared.

Preparation of surfaces need not be a chore. In fact, most painters find it an enjoyable task. Not only is it exciting to see a surface being readied, but it can be prepared to feature exactly the right amount of texture and absorbency which suits your painting style.

THE IMPACT OF SURFACES ON PAINTING

It is a wonderful experience to sit among a large group of people who are learning to paint. Much is learnt from watching others and in so doing, one realises that all newcomers experience the same basic problems and what needs to be understood is that these problems are not down to lack of talent.

When looking around such a group, it becomes evident that there is something different in the way the paint works for each and every one. The individual style of working is not the cause of this diversity; rather, it is the physical manner in which the paint is reacting.

It seems strange that some painters produce brush-strokes that are fluid and shiny, while others seem to be struggling with a swiftly drying and stubborn surface. However, the reason is so simple that most miss it completely. Generally, we all too readily blame ourselves for the way the paint reacts, when in fact the disparities are due to the different surfaces on which everyone is working.

Some surfaces are absorbing the paint like blotting paper and on others the paint is remaining wet. Whereas everyone is using a ground recommended for oil painting, the differences are only now becoming evident.

What is happening here?
Since there are many ways in which to prepare a ground and so many possible bases, it stands to reason that resultant absorbencies will also differ.

Each will therefore have a unique feel and respond differently as the first washy strokes of oil paint are applied. Whilst all grounds are equally acceptable, the choice of which to use is down to individual taste and painting style.

Once the first layers have been painted and you have moved on to layering paint on paint, the surface is less absorbent. At this stage it is the texture of the surface that makes the difference.

It is imperative to understand how the physical differences of the ground will ultimately determine the finished result of any painting. Oil painting is a little like a game of chess. Make the wrong move at the beginning and the game could be lost, even if played well. Time and effort put into making the right preparations from the start will pay dividends.

SELECTING YOUR GROUND

The cheapest ground for oil sketching is oil paper. This come in two forms – one a paper, the other very thin canvas and as you would expect, paper and canvas are physically different. The paper option is generally available in rough, medium and smooth finishes.

Oil paper is usually primed with a layer of acrylic paint, an ideal ground that prevents much of the oil being absorbed. This enables subsequently applied oil paint to grip the resultant stable, strong surface.

Acrylic also strengthens the base and fixes any irregularities present in the surface over which it is painted. Both the paper and the canvas bases benefit from the acrylic. However, the canvas, being naturally more absorbent, will remain so, even after the acrylic layer has been applied.

Again the choice of which to use is an individual one and so it is when deciding whether or not to use canvas boards, or for that matter canvas itself. Both

the original texture of the ground and the absorbency of each need to be taken into account, when deciding which is more suitable for your individual needs.

PREPARING YOUR SURFACES

Since many painters enjoy preparing grounds unique to their own style, it is important to know the difference between sizing and priming and how to go about each.

It is also necessary to fully appreciate how the different finishes that can be applied to the ground will ultimately determine the finished result of your painting. The exercise in this section will help you experience how the physical nature of a few simple textures can be exploited to great effect.

> **TERMS:**
> **Base** - the initial, unprepared surface.
> **Ground** - the prepared surface on which the painting is commenced.
> **Surface** - the layer of paint on which further paint is being applied at any stage.

Understanding surfaces

ARTSTRIPS ©

Most bases will absorb the medium (oil) from the paint causing dullness and cracking unless suitably prepared.

Ready-made (prepared) grounds are available. [from top] - oil paper (for sketching), oil board (oil paper on board), canvas board, stretched canvas.

Preparing your own ground involves - (1) SIZING, to plug any surface 'pores' or 'weaves'.

(2) Once dry, PRIMING, to apply a layer impervious to the oil.

Cheap alternative - (1) Size with two layers of wallpaper paste. Dry out and sand between layers.

(2) Use wide decorating brush to prime with three layers of thinned emulsion paint. Dry and sand between layers as before.

Traditional method - (1) Apply size of rabbit-skin glue, available in granular form. Dissolve in hot water, cool and apply two layers.

(2) Prime with one of the many available brands of acrylic primer, or acrylic gesso primer, or oil painting primer.

Gently sand between layers, using circular motion. Wrap sandpaper around small block of wood for heavier sanding.

Surfaces in practice

Preparing your own ground - Sizing

Oil painting can be applied to almost any base, as long as it is reasonably stable so as not to cause cracking within hard paint layers. To ensure bases will not absorb the oil from the paint, thus weakening their structure, they must be first sized and then primed.

Sizing

Sizing is simply a means of filling the pores, holes or weave of the surface. This provides a stable layer on which to apply the primer, thus ensuring a stable ground for the oil paint.

A cheaper alternative when starting out is to utilise a solution of household wallpaper paste, mixed as specified on the packet. Because any loose hairs or dust particles become trapped in this layer of size, it is important to sand these off, before applying a second layer of size.

  The traditional method for sizing follows the same steps, using a solution of rabbit-skin glue. Available in granular form, it is made into a solution with the addition of hot water and it is advisable to only make up enough for immediate use. The solution soon begins to go off; resulting in an unpleasant smell and it goes without saying that immediate disposal of any excess solution is desirable.

STARTING OFF

Oil paper is the perfect solution for oil sketching or first attempts. This is a textured paper that has been already primed with acrylic. Available in a variety of finishes, from 'fine' to 'rough' to best mimic canvas. As the primer has been applied to only one side, it is essential that this side is painted on.

When bought in the form of a pad, the correct surface faces upward. The primed face of loose sheets usually features a creamier coloration than the incorrect reverse. Other defining features can include a darker brown coloration, or the maker's name. Should a firmer ground be preferred, move on to ready-to-use oil boards, or canvas boards.

TIP:

In a hurry? Size and prime with thin washes of acrylic medium. This soaks into the surface and when dry, is tough, flexible and colourless. Immediately after applications, wash brushes carefully to avoid damage.

Surfaces in practice

Preparing your own ground - Priming

Once sized, the surface is then primed to make it less absorbent to the oil in the paint. As it is the oil which, when dry, fixes the pigment in place, any absorption by the surface will render the paint liable to damage. The oil absorbed into the ground can prove unsightly and can actually cause its disintegration over time. Surface shine will be lost as the oil sinks out of view and visually this will cause a loss of depth to the colour.

Priming options

OIL PAINTING PRIMER
Available as ready-to-use Alkyd (oil resin) based fluid, mixed with white pigment, this produces a thixotropic (glutinous) white layer that does not require thinning. Although the treated base will be unlikely to absorb the primer, it is usually necessary to apply two or three layers to achieve the desired smooth surface. Each coat will require approximately twenty-four hours to dry and can be sanded gently before applying the subsequent coat. For coloured grounds, a small amount of oil colour is added to the primer to suit personal taste. On thin bases, such as card or hardboard, it is advisable to paint the reverse side, or at least a cross shape of primer to counteract warping.

ACRYLIC GESSO PRIMER
Gesso (plaster of Paris/gypsum) mixed with acrylic resin (medium), which produces an opaque and fast drying primer. It can be used on a wide variety of surfaces and will serve as a primer for both oil and acrylic painting. Acrylic primers really have improved over the years, becoming much more solid in colour, while retaining the flexibility of an acrylic, once dry. Available in black or white - the choice being how dark or light the preferred underpainting. Clear Gesso Base is also available and can be coloured with acrylic paint to suit personal taste and provides all the qualities of texture and absorbency required to prime a variety of bases.

FOUNDATION WHITE
Excellent as an oil-based primer for oil painting, it can be thinned with any oil painting thinner for smooth application. While each layer will be touch-dry overnight, being oil-based, it should be left for several days to dry thoroughly before beginning to paint.

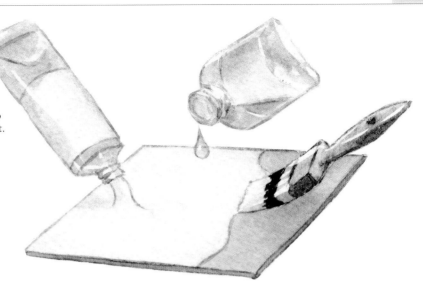

TIP:

Preparing the ground is a vital aspect of the oil painting technique. It ensures ease of paint application and longevity of dried paint layers. As can be seen however, preparing grounds does take time, so it is well worth preparing several canvasses or boards at the same time.

UNDERPAINTING WHITE
A much stiffer, fast-drying paint, with a flat matt finish when dry. Excellent for creating a textured surface on which to start your painting. This texture can be arbitrary, to simply break up brush-strokes, or structural, echoing the forms within the composition.

NOTES

• Apply primers with a large, flat, bristle brush.

• Several thin layers are preferable to one thick one.

• It is advisable to sand each dried application, which produces a smooth surface on which to paint.

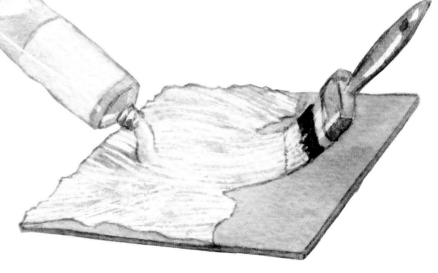

Exercise for surfaces

Sky and moss - canvas surface weave - Use a soft round nylon brush and fluid colour mixes (alkyd medium and thinner) to brush directly onto the primed canvas ground. The texture is immediately revealed. Use a round bristle brush and tube consistency paint to scuff over the lighter values. These lights lie on the raised relief of the canvas - a complete contrast to the accents created by the previous fluid mix.

Lying stones - smooth surface - With a painting knife and stiff white paint, create a veneer of paint that almost completely obscures the canvas texture beneath. Once dry, overpaint using a large soft round brush and dark colour mixes, to which a little alkyd medium has been added, to effect soft blended strokes. Build lighter values on top of the darks.

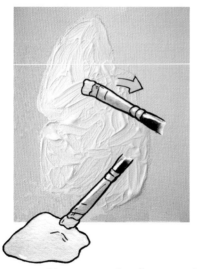

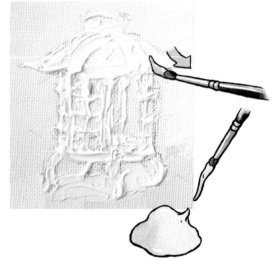

Standing stones - arbitrary textured surface - Use a flat bristle brush throughout and stiff white colour, to apply strokes in all directions. Once dry, apply a fluid dark under-painting (alkyd medium). Allow to dry, and then overpaint with tube consistency colour. Build toward light colours - cool in shadow areas and warm in sunlight. The lower colours are brushed in the same direction as the underlying textures to achieve good coverage. Final highlight is brushed across the strokes for extra contrast.

Oriental lamp - structured texture surface - Turn to a small nylon round brush and thick impasto white paint to draw around and describe the form of the lamp. Once dry, flood the textures with dark colour. Allow to dry, before building dark to light colours, with tube consistency paint.

Surface preparation can be exploited to have a direct effect on the finish of the top layers of colour. The canvas weave itself offers an interesting texture, as can be seen in the areas of sky and mossy banks of this study. Three other areas are treated quite differently to demonstrate further effects of texture.

In one, the texture is completely flattened by applying stiff white paint with a palette knife. Although this could be carried out with oil paint, you might like to try acrylic texture paste, as was used in this exercise.

Whilst acrylic texture paste dries much faster, it has to be applied more generously. Acrylic shrinks on drying and the canvas texture is likely to come through, if the texture paste is applied too thinly.

Vigorously applied brush textures feature on the standing stone and the lamp. This introduces the notion that the surface itself can be re-invented and restructured as part of the painting process - as further demonstrated in the accompanying project.

Is it strictly necessary to understand colour mixing, when almost every colour is available as a pre-mixed paint?

This is a very pertinent question and in no way implies laziness on the part of the person asking it. After all, there are so many other things to think about and it would seem reasonable to avail oneself of a range of pre-mixed colours.

TO ENABLE THAT DECISION TO BE MADE in the first place requires knowledge of colour mixing. It is only through understanding the basics of mixing colour that an artist can fully appreciate how important a role it plays in the painting process. Furthermore, it is only through studying and experiencing the function of colour in a composition that any painter can appreciate and exploit the subtleties of colour this demands.

Take the human face for example. Whilst it is possible to obtain a tube of 'flesh' colour, what precisely will this contain? After all, there are young faces and old, male and female, notwithstanding the fact that every person in the world has a skin colour unique to themselves.

And it does not stop there; every face is made up of a multitude of different hues and values and if the light changes, even slightly, those hues and values all change with it. If one tube of colour could deliver all of these attributes it certainly would be worth every penny.

There is no getting away from the fact that every artist should know how colour works and the good news is that not only is colour mixing based on a simple system, it is also very enjoyable to discover. To understand colour, is to open up a more interesting world around you.

The aim of this section is to remove any fear you may already have of mixing colours, or for that matter the concern you may have of getting to grips with it as a complete beginner.

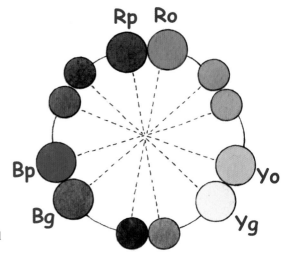

> **TIP**:
>
> Always go for the larger tubes of oil paint, they work out cheaper in the long run. Aim to have a basic palette of colours in large tubes, rather than a wide range of colours in small tubes.

There are two benefits in gaining the experience required to exploit colour mixing to its fullest, the first being how to achieve a specific colour. To do this you must look at the colour in question and establish three things. What is its hue, how dark or light is its value and lastly, what is its intensity or brightness [*chroma*]?

1. All hues can be identified along the outer ring of the colour circle.

2. The value of a colour can be darkened by adding a colour of darker value or its complementary colour found across from it on the colour circle. To lighten it white is added.

3. Colours around the outer ring of the colour circle are bright, but move toward grey or black as their complementaries are added towards the centre.

Once the knowledge of how to mix specific colours has been gained, you will be able to control the balance of colours across the whole of any composition.

The second benefit is the practical aspect of how paint colours physically work on the palette surface. How can they be controlled so that the volume of paint mix is sufficient? How best to load them onto brush or knife to maximise the brush–stroke? Is it best to mix with brush or knife?

COLOUR REFERENCE	**COLOUR MIXING**
Red-purple [Rp] Red-orange [Ro] Blue-purple [Bp] Blue-green [Bg] Yellow-orange [Yo] Yellow-green [Yg] Underpainting White [UW] Titanium White [TW] Zinc White [ZW]	Where the pre-fix letter is shown in capitals this denotes a larger quantity of that particular colour. Conversely, where the pre-fix letter is shown in a lower case, this denotes a smaller quantity of that particular colour. Example: Bp = **large** amount of blue-purple bp = **small** amount of blue-purple

OIL PAINTING COLOUR PALETTE

In oil painting it is really important to start with a palette of basic colours and get to know them intimately. There is not only the cost of having a wide range of colours to consider, but tubes of oil paint are heavy and the more you have the more awkward they are to transport.

All of the exercises and projects in this book are produced with a basic palette of six colours, plus the addition of three whites. This makes handling the paint on the palette far simpler as well, for in using the palette properly the process of painting will run a great deal more smoothly.

Ideally your paints should be laid out on the outer rim of the palette in an order that reflects the natural layout of colours on the colour circle. This will allow you instant access to your colours when producing mixes on the palette.

TIP:

When following the tuition in this book, rather than just accepting a suggested colour mix, consider what is behind that suggestion. Work out how the mix is functioning and if it does not happen the first time, resolve to find out why it failed. Just as much can be learnt from failures in colour mixing as can be from successes.

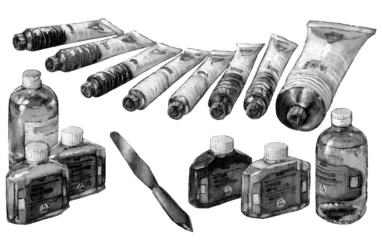

PRIMARY COLOURS cannot be achieved through mixing. Instead are used in mixes to achieve other colours.

In theory - primary colours are mixed to create secondary colours.

Sometimes this just does not seem to work, because...

...more than one set of primaries are required. Ones that are biased to the secondary colours they mix best.

From which can be created bright secondaries...

...or dull secondaries.

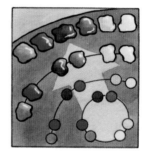

PALETTE MIXING - the colour circle is flattened out with each colour retaining its position to make identification and mixing easier

Mixing colours that are close produces bright secondary colours.

Mixing colours that are more distant produces dull secondary colours.

TAKE CARE : Some colours are more powerful in mixtures (tinting strength). Adding equal amounts does not always yield the expected result.

By adjusting quantities, a middle secondary is achieved.

Mixture is controlled by adding just a little of the strong colour to the edge of the weaker mix.

Palette mixing

BRIGHT SECONDARY MIXES

Mixing primaries next to one another on the colour circle creates intense (bright) secondary mixes.

Red-orange [Ro] +Yellow-orange [Yo] make a good orange, both having an orange bias. The mix varies around their shape - Red being darker in value suggests the shadow when predominant in the mixture.

The purple grapes are mixed from Red-purple [Rp] + Blue-purple [Bp]. As both colours are dark in value, white needs to be added, as well as varying the hue - to create volume. Note how the addition of white also dulls the intensity.

The green of the apples, while both being mixed from Blue-green [Bg] + Yellow-green [Yg] appear to be different.

This simple change is made by adding more yellow to the fruit in the foreground and more blue to the one behind. Again, the darker hue is more predominant in the shadows.

DULL SECONDARY MIXES

These mixes are created by using primaries at the furthest distance from each other, with a bias away from the secondary colour for which they have been chosen to mix.

The orange is therefore mixed from Yellow-green [Yg] + Red-purple [Rp].

The grapes are Red-orange [Ro] + Blue-green [Bg], while the apples are a mix of Blue-purple [Bp] + Yellow-orange [Yo]. As in the first illustration, the grapes have white added to create the necessary lights and highlights, which suggest volume.

Again, the apples have either more yellow (front) or more blue (back) in their mix.

Note how grey the grapes have become and while the orange is probably the brightest of the mixes, compare it with the bright orange of close primaries in the first example.

Exercise

BRIGHT SECONDARY MIXES

The bottom half of this exercise is painted in all of the bright secondary colours. In the diagram the differing sizes of each circle is used to indicate that the quantity of each pigment varies in line with the tinting strength of the paint used in the mix. For instance, there are six greens, each made from Blue-green [Bg] and Yellow-green [Yg]. In all cases, the amount of [Bg] remains relatively small, as it is such a powerful colour in the mix. With these six mixes alone you can get a taste of the variety of possibilities available and how the addition of white makes such a difference. Note especially the dulling nature of white. All of the light colours tend toward dullness and should their intensity disappoint, will require glazing, to restore their richness.

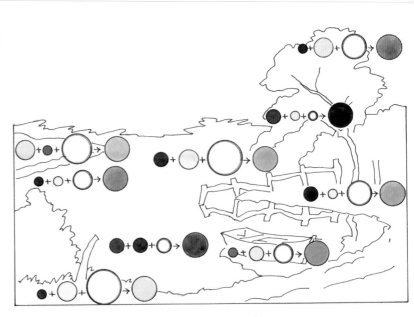

DULL SECONDARY MIXES

The top half of the exercise is painted using dull secondary mixes. While the exercise has been very strictly controlled to employ only distant primaries, you can be a little more lenient when mixing in practice. For example, the distant hills are painted with a mix of Blue-purple [Bp] and Yellow-orange [Yo]. Both have a bias away from green and this creates a very dull secondary. However, you could use a primary with the bias to green, along with a primary without that bias. Try for yourself a mix of Blue-green [Bg] and Yellow-orange [Yo], as well as a mix of Blue-purple [Bp] and Yellow-green [Yg].

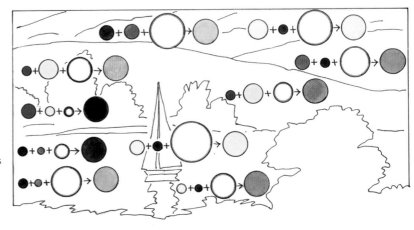

NOTE

GIVEN THAT YOU CAN ALSO VARY THE AMOUNT OF EACH HUE AND THE QUANTITIES OF WHITE, YOU BEGIN TO REALISE THE RANGE OF MIXES AVAILABLE AS SECONDARIES.

This exercise is painted directly onto a white surface using undiluted tube colour. In this way, colours will not be affected by any underpainting and will also remain separate on the surface, rather than mixing into one another.

All of the colours used are created as secondary mixes, but those produced for the top half of the study are dull, while those mixed for the bottom half are bright. This is accomplished by invoking close primary mixes for the bottom and distant primary mixes for the top, in order to achieve the required secondary colours.

The resultant duller colours in the distance immediately suggest depth, by displaying a natural characteristic of the phenomenon known as aerial perspective. This is when distant colour is leached away, because it travels the furthest distance through the atmosphere to reach the viewer. The effect is aided by softer edges in the distance and a smaller range of values, when compared to the brushy contrasts of the foreground.

NOTE

ADD COLOUR TO A PALETTE MIX BY INTRODUCING IT FROM THE SIDE, RATHER THAN ADDING TO THE CENTRE. THIS ALLOWS FOR CONTROL OVER EXACTLY HOW MUCH OF EACH IS USED, WITHOUT MIXES GOING AWRY AND BECOMING INCREASINGLY LARGER.

ESPECIALLY IMPORTANT WHEN ADDING WHITE, AS SOME HUES, BEING VERY POWERFUL, WOULD DEMAND ENORMOUS AMOUNTS OF WHITE, WERE IT TO BE ADDED TO THE WHOLE MIX.

Common problems

PROBLEM

Most painters experimenting with oil paints for the first time are often frustrated with the medium drying too fast or too slow. This frustration spills over into what to do with paint left over from a painting session, or how to preserve the paint on a palette for future use. After all, no-one wants to throw away valuable paint at the end of a session. However, once the mechanics of drying are understood, this problem can be easily overcome in a number of ways.

HOW OIL PAINTS DRY

Oil paint generally dries by chemical reaction and not by evaporation. When the medium (oil) in the paint is exposed to the air, the two react, causing the oil to stiffen and eventually harden. Oil paint dries very hard on the palette surface and you can soon end up with paint that seems welded in place. The flow of air over the palette needs to be restricted, to prevent this from occurring.

SOLUTION

A – One option is to cover the paint with transparent food wrapping. This however can be a little messy when you have to remove it again.
B – Alternatively, place the palette in a cardboard box covered with a lid.
C – Canvas Carriers are useful in restricting airflow and preventing surface contact. This is my preferred method, as it also provides an excellent way in which to transport a wet palette.
D – Submerging the palette in water eliminates air and as oils and water do not mix, the paint stays in place.
E – One of the simplest methods in the studio is to lean both palette and painting against a wall. This can be quite effective for short periods of a few days.

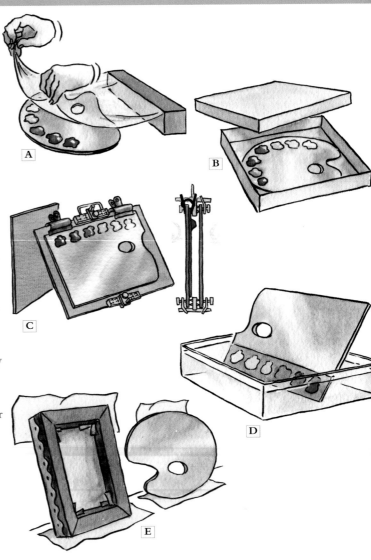

PREVENTING THE SURFACE OF A PALETTE FROM BECOMING PAINT HARDENED

MISTAKE

F – Scraping off dried paint can cause damage to the palette surface, even to the point of removing the varnish that coats the palette. This results in the oil from subsequently squeezed out paint being absorbed into the surface of what has now become an absorbent palette. Whilst still usable, the paint will consequently be duller and weaker as the medium (oil) that holds it together and to the canvas, will have been reduced in volume.

REMEDY

G – Keep the fresh tube colour along the outer edge of the palette and mix in the centre.

H – At the end of a session use your palette knife to remove the paint mixes from the central area.

J – Use a lint free rag to remove the small amount of remaining paint and polish up the mixing area with the same cloth.

NOTE

THROUGHOUT EACH PAINTING SESSION A SMALL AMOUNT OF OIL PENETRATES THE WOODEN SURFACE AND SOON YOU WILL HAVE A SMOOTH, GLOSSY SURFACE ON WHICH TO MIX COLOURS. TO AID THE PENETRATION OF OIL INTO THE WOODEN SURFACE WHEN DOING THIS, AVOID USING TURPENTINE OR ANY THINNER TO DISSOLVE SURFACE PAINT.

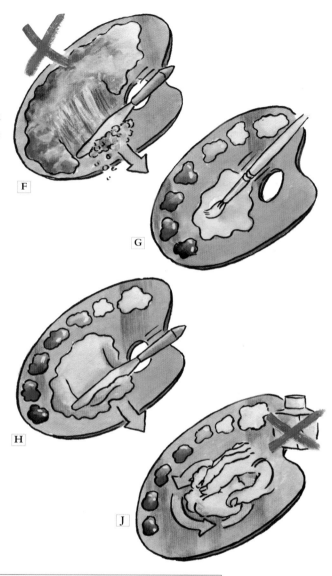

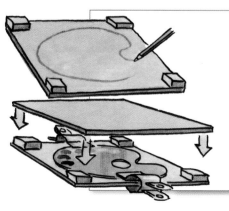

TIP:

An alternative method to canvas carriers for storing your palette
Draw out the shape of your palette on a piece of hardboard cut to size. Glue wooden blocks to its corners. Use bulldog clips to hold the palette in place. Cover with a second piece of hardboard and hold together with a strong elastic band.

Underpainting mixes

To draw out in colour use fluid mix with plenty of thinner.

Draw in large areas of composition from reference material. Keep shapes simple

A little detail may be added. Go too far and you will be reluctant to be bold with application of underpainting.

Keep colour mixes dark and dull. Add enough thinner to keep fluid, but not so much as to cause running.

Use large round bristle brush to block in. Thinner will swiftly evaporate to leave very thin layer of pigment and oil, which will dry dull.

Underpainting can simply comprise of colours that are dull, dark equivalents of final colours...

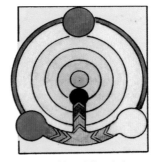

...achieved by adding their complementary colour. E.G. - to green add a touch of opposite red to produce dull dark green.

Extra contrast is available by employing underpainting comprising of dull colours complementary to the final colours...

...achieved by using mixes further across colour circle. E.G. - to greens add more red to produce dull dark red.

Or...you can be even bolder and go the whole way...

...by underpainting in bright complementaries. E.G. - use bright reds as an underpainting colour for greens.

Accents of complementary underpainting colour left between strokes of overpainting create contrasts that make final colours appear brighter.

Exercise

The main purpose of the underpainting layer is to cover the surface with colour, so that the predominant masses of the composition can be seen in place for the first time. It is the final chance to make up your mind as to whether or not the composition holds together well at the size in which you intend it to be completed.

Underpainting with darker, duller versions of final colours

This approach to underpainting is that with which most painters would probably associate; painting colours that are a darker, duller version of the final colours to provide very natural dark accents in the finished painting. While the underpainting layer is a little dismal, at least one can see the direction in which the painting is going to move, as the layers are built on top. Since the colours are dull and uninspiring at this stage, it is easy to make substantial changes, should they be necessary.

These dark, dull mixes are created using complementaries. For example, note how the sky, which will eventually be painted yellow, is first painted a dull mid-brown. To achieve this, establish the position of the yellow on the colour circle and travel directly across the circle, to discover its complementary. The opposite of Yellow-orange [Yo] is therefore a purple blue, referred to as Blue-purple [Bp], for the primary colour is named first.

Adding the Blue-purple will make the colour darker and duller, as it theoretically moves towards black. Since this black is always a dark colour, it is more sensible to think of this as a dark, coloured grey. Stopping before this coloured grey is reached gives us a dull version of the colour with which we began. Treat all the colours in this manner and complete the underpainting.

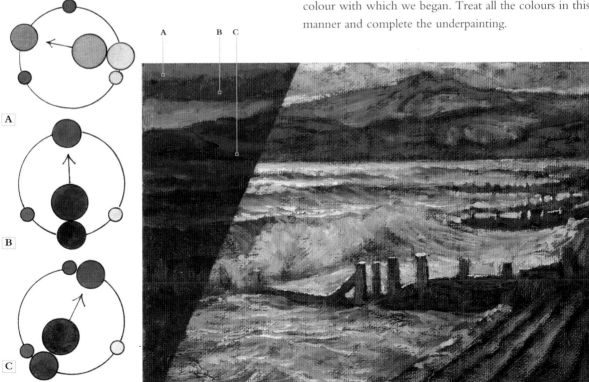

Exercise

Underpainting with dull complementary colours

In the first exercise, different values of the same colour were used to provide a contrast against one another. Basically, this means the painting was built from dark to light. The dark colours become the natural colours of shadows as the painting moves toward light.

Now move on to more fully exploit colour. Instead of simply changing the value, the hue of the colour will also change, as it builds in thickness. Again the complementaries are to be exploited. However, to establish the correct under-colours, you have to move through the neutral centre of the colour circle and on to the other side.

Revisiting the sky, a light Yellow-orange [Yo] is to be its colour in the final layer.. For the underpainting, Blue-purple [Bp] is gradually added as before and the colour will darken and lose intensity until it becomes almost black. This point of the mix will prove interesting, as you will discover several colours of black

along the way. Eventually, as more Blue-purple is added the mix will move through the mid point of the colour circle, until it emerges as a very dark dull Blue-purple. Adding white to this will bring it a little closer in value to the original Yellow-orange, but the mix is kept several degrees darker so that the value contrast is preserved.

All the other colours should be treated in the same way, by discovering their complementaries until the underpainting is completed. The result is a generally warm, dull underpainting - an exact opposite to the cool hues of the final painting. When you get used to the colour negative effect, the underpainting will become easier to live with.

As soon as you begin to apply the true colours, the results are electrifying. Colour is now seen against colour, as well as value and the contrasting hues begin to sing out. Once you have tried this approach you will begin to love underpainting and really enjoy your colour palette.

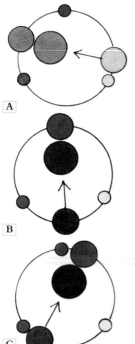

A

B

C

A   B C

Underpainting with bright complementary colours

Having whetted your appetite for complementary underpainting, now you should push forward into something really exciting. Have you ever looked at an Impressionists' painting with a grey sky and wondered how it seems so full of colour? The answer is more than likely to lie in the underpainting. Look below the grey sky at the colour beneath the brush-strokes.

It is probable that a vivid colour lies underneath. Although the underlying colours may only show through a fraction of the over-painting, these tiny accents excite our retina and affect the large mass of grey, which we in turn read as a colour.

These colours are known as complementary contrasts or accents and to achieve them you again need to place the final colours of the composition on the colour circle and travel right across to their opposites. These complementaries are painted directly on the surface as the underpainting, unsullied by any mixing.

The effect is startling and you may find it difficult to live with. I have witnessed the disbelief on the faces of painters trying this for the first time. When faced with the suggestion that a grassy hill should be underpainted in bright red, it takes some faith to take me at my word.

However, the effects are simply stunning when these colours are subsequently over-painted. Some depth is inevitably lost, in comparison to the previous methods, but the surface resonates with colour.

You will probably be tempted to leave more of the underpainting exposed, which only serves to heighten the drama. Certainly the effect begins to look more painterly and you will probably find that some subjects, more than others, suit the approach. However it is a marvellous way in which to start a painting and gets the adrenaline going, whatever your temperament.

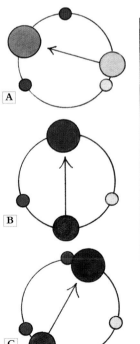

Common problems

PROBLEM

Adding a thinner to paint makes the job fast and efficient when applying the underpainting. However, there is a down side to thinning paint. The first being that too fluid a surface can cause paint runs. It can also make it difficult to apply subsequent, heavier paint layers. You need to balance the amount of thinner carefully, so that the paint will flow, but not swamp the surface.

PROTECTING VULNERABLE AREAS OF PAINT

A - Adding thinner spreads out both the pigment and the oil. Since the oil is the glue that sticks the pigment to the surface, it stands to reason that in spreading it you are substantially weakening the paint layer.

B - Once the thinner has evaporated away the pigment is left high and dry, with only a modicum of oil to stick it fast. Overworking of the surface will create enough friction to dislodge the colour. While you are over-painting with generous amounts of paint, as layering demands, this will not cause a problem. However, problems can occur when the surface is brushed vigorously.

C - During glazing for example, areas of underpainting left between heavier brush-strokes, are vulnerable to over enthusiastic brushing. When this occurs the underpainting will dislodge and begin to sully the purity of the glaze. There are two solutions to the problem and they are best used in tandem.

D - First, be gentle in the application of glazes. The function of a glaze is to run naturally into the impasto texture of the paint. If it is found that more pressure is required to apply the glaze, it is probably best to switch to a slightly more fluid, glazing medium. Alkyd glazing mediums are available in up to four different fluidities.

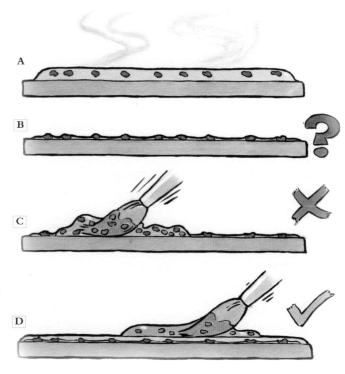

The second approach is to employ retouching varnish, which can be used at any stage of a painting, provided the surface is dry. This acts as a temporary seal and will help to prevent the vulnerable pigment from lifting off as you work.

RESTORING DULLED AREAS OF PAINT

A - Making the paint fluid with thinner can produce exciting results. So much so, that some painters stop at this early stage. Whilst there is no reason to find fault in this approach, there is much more yet to explore, before the full potential of oil painting has been reached.

However, you may prefer to allow the paint layer to dry first at this stage, before continuing with the heavier colour.

B - What you may well find when returning to the painting is that the surface has become very dull. Even if you had continued, any small areas of underpainting left between brush-strokes would, likewise, have become dull. As colours become dull they lose their lustre and depth. Accents require this richness and so a dull underpainting simply will not do. The cause of the dullness? The thinner used to make the paint fluid also thinned out the medium (oil) in the paint. Since it is the oil which makes the paint shine, thinning it out renders the oil ineffective.

C - Restoration of this shine is referred to as 'oiling out' and is accomplished by using a varnish. However, it is essential to ensure the correct varnish is selected for this job.

FINISHING VARNISHES – when applied to the surface these produce a protective seal against the atmosphere and the paint can only dry if the air can get to it.

RETOUCHING VARNISHES – allow the air to pass through to the paint beneath, which means that as soon as the surface is dry, a thin layer can be applied. This must be done in broad strokes, using a large flat brush. Varnishing the painting in this manner will immediately restore the shine and thus the contrasts necessary to your composition.

NOTE - Although retouching varnish dries swiftly, it is possible to paint into it while still wet. For those who prefer to paint wet-into-wet, it is a way of making the surface wet, whilst ensuring the colour beneath is relatively fixed in place. Providing that brush-strokes on top are kept gentle.

Layer mixing

HOW COLOUR MIXES ARE USED IN ASCENDING LAYERS

Oil painting is layered naturally, working on the premise of lean to fat, thick to thin. In other words, as the layers are built in depth, so the amount of oil in the paint increases. However, as the layers are built over each other it is difficult to visualise the colour mixing and colour relationships at each individual stage. In order to best fix these in your mind the following exercises treat each layer as a separate entity. First, we see underpainting, then impasto. Layered paint is then investigated and finally glazing. Each layer is painted using only one brush – a medium to small, long-headed round bristle.

EXERCISE 1
FIRST LAYER - UNDERPAINTING
DARK and FLAT

The simplest way of creating the dark colours required for the underpainting is to add their complementaries. By also thinning the mix with the addition of turpentine substitute or white spirit, this layer becomes very smooth and dries swiftly [Fig. A]. The addition of turpentine substitute also makes the colours appear very dull when dry. Only a small amount of this underpainting will be seen on the finished painting, providing dark accents for the overlaid lighter, brighter colours.

COMPLEMENTARIES - Colour mixes move from both cool and warm greens towards the centre of the colour circle, with the addition of their complementary reds. In this exercise they become dull, dark, grey greens.

Fig. A

EXERCISE 2
SECOND LAYER - IMPASTO 'STIFF' TUBE PAINT
LIGHT and TEXTURED

One of the most important aspects of this layer is the creation of texture, *impasto* [Fig. B]. To speed up the drying of this layer we use underpainting white in the mixes. This white dries swiftly and is less likely to crack than other whites, when used heavily. The lighter and more deeply textured these strokes become, the more successful the overlaid glazes are likely to be. In this exercise, all possible underpainting colours have been replaced by one flat colour [top left], for enhanced definition of overlaid impasto.

Fig. B

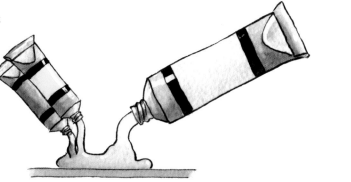

TINTS (COLOUR plus WHITE) - Use underpainting white in the colour mixes to create stiff, heavily textured layer.

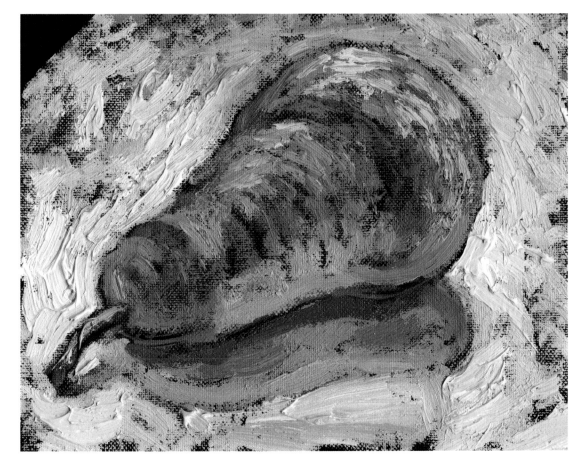

EXERCISE 3
SECOND LAYER (alternative) - 'STIFF' TUBE PAINT
DARK to LIGHT

The stiffness of colour taken directly from the tube, not only allows you to create impasto paint, but also to build layers from dark to light. This creates all the

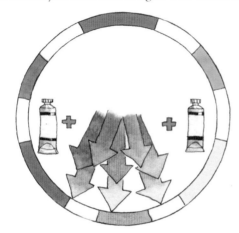

modelling of light required to suggest volume [Fig C] and can be left as is (alla prima). Alternatively it can be enhanced with glazing when dry (at the next stage). In this exercise, the paint was applied over one flat colour [top left] so that the colour changes would not be confused with those of the underpainting.

In this exercise the green mixes move from dull grey greens near the centre of the colour circle and are made lighter (by adding white) and brighter (by adding colour from the outside of the colour circle).

Fig. C

EXERCISE 4
TOP LAYER - GLAZES
LIGHT to DARK

Fig. D

Return to the previously completed Exercise 2, which you can now over-paint with transparent glazes [Fig. D]. These will bring richness and depth of colour and enhance the textures already present in the thick impasto layer. Mixing or layering glazes of the same colour family as the impasto layer will slowly intensify and darken the colours. [top of fruit]. Mixing or layering glazes of opposite (complementary) colours to the impasto layer will slowly dull and darken the colours (bottom of fruit).

Glazes can be mixed on the palette or on the painting surface. You could wait for one layer of glaze to dry before applying the next. Alternatively, apply a small amount of tube colour directly into a wet glaze and work it into the wet surface.

Common problems

PROBLEM

Glazing is such an exciting technique that it is very common to be over generous in its application. Glazes add to the richness of a colour and they bring out its textures in a way that is unique amongst all of the media. They also always darken the colour, even when applied very gently. Thus, the more layers of glaze, the darker the overall values become.

REMOVING UNWANTED GLAZES

Even when created with alkyd mediums, glazes take a while to dry, which allows you time to deliberate and decide whether the correct choice has been made. This also affords the added advantage of being able to try something out, even when you may be dubious as to the outcome, because a wrongly applied glaze can ultimately be removed while still wet.

METHOD

Find a light area of textured colour on a painting, which you feel might benefit from glazing. Remember that the colour can be enriched through adding a glaze of the same family, or dulled by over-glazing with a complementary. Apply a generous glaze, in both a very fluid form and a stiff mix, by adding more or less paint and experimenting with different fluidities of glazing medium.

To progressively remove the glaze...

1 - Gently rub over the surface using the end of a finger. Note how this lifts the glaze from the most prominent parts of the surface relief, leaving it in the depressions.

2 - For a more aggressive approach, use a lint-free rag, which lifts the glaze deeper out of the furrows. A tissue is useless, as the rough texture will tear it to shreds and particles will become lodged in the glaze.

3 - Damp the lint-free rag, or gently dampen a brush with thinner - wipe across the surface.

4 - Alternatively, try substituting the thinner with some clean glazing medium for removal with a brush (note flat angle of the brush).

5 - To fully remove the glaze, increase the angle of the brush and the amount of thinner it contains. Work vigorously into the textures and wipe clean with a cloth.

NOTE - when this dries, the thinner will have made the area very dull. Oil out with retouching varnish before continuing to paint.

TIP:

Before removing a glaze completely, try a partial removal, as this can lead to some surprising and exciting results.

Discovering paint qualities

Oil painting is probably the most versatile of all of the painting mediums. Every artist discovers, or should I say, rediscovers, a different aspect for themselves. The paint can be used thin or thick, in its pure form or diluted with thinners or oils. In fact, each layer of the painting can have paints of differing consistencies.

In this section oil paint is explored in its rawest form - straight from the tube - in which it displays its true character. Thick, juicy and rich in pigment, the paint glows on the palette, inviting a bold approach in its application.

THERE IS NO MORE EXCITING A METHOD than to use a painting knife. Whilst working with a painting knife may at first appear crude, it is only through trying it out that the subtleties of the technique can be appreciated. By sticking to this one implement, you will also be able to concentrate on the nature of the paint, with which you are working. It gives you a chance to get the true feel for paint.

Admittedly the first experience of painting with a painting knife may force you to rely on suggestion rather than detail. You may have to loosen up your approach and put some rhythm into the painting strokes. But is this not what painting is all about, the discovery of new techniques and first-time experiences?

Certainly it will prove an essential experience and even if it does not become one of your central techniques, working with a painting knife will most certainly come into its own for certain passages, where you need its particular qualities.

There is nothing that executes rock and stone cliff faces quite so dramatically as the painting knife. It is even possible to apply a thick glaze over rough texture using a knife laden with a transparent gel-like glaze, comprising of paint and thick alkyd medium.

The possibilities are endless, but to make them possible you must learn to get the best out of this tool.

However, let me first overcome the confusion inherent in calling this technique by its more generally accepted term of 'palette knife' painting. A palette knife is shaped specifically for mixing paint on the palette, as well as for cleaning it off. The results of painting with this implement would be very disappointing and it should be kept solely for its original purpose.

Painting knives, on the other hand, are trowel-shaped and provide the correct angle needed to apply paint to the painting surface. These knives are flexible, far more suited for the job of painting and come in a multitude of shapes and sizes. Just as you would build up a collection of brushes for different techniques and effects, so too would a range of painting knives prove useful.

There is an immediacy about palette knife painting, which is both challenging and enthralling. You will often find yourself holding your breath as you make bold moves. The exciting results are worth it however and in the process any fear of working with stiff paint will have definitely been overcome.

ARTSTRIPS©

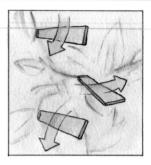

STEP 1 - Cut painting spatulas from old piece of cardboard. Discarded backboards of sketchbooks are excellent.

Prepare a stiff painting surface. Apply thin wash [thinner + oil paint] over surface with a bristle brush.

Mix blue grey with wide end of spatula [top] - no medium added. Dip in narrow end [bottom]...

...and draw rhythmic shapes of composition into still-wet, coloured wash.

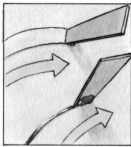

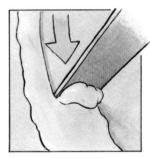

STEP 2 - Mix ample quantities of paint to load spatula generously.

Experiment with stroke in different directions and vary pressure during application.

Clean spatulas between colours - wipe with clean tissue or cotton rag.

Scrape off excess paint from surface with clean spatula.

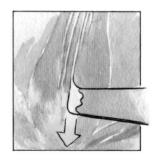

STEP 3 - Heavy loading [top] drips paint that can be dropped and dragged across surface [bottom].

Deposit heavy colour [top]. Blend with clean spatula [bottom].

Heavily load paint and drag card, edge-on, to create ridges.

Create fine line over heavy colour by dabbing with frequently reloaded, dripping spatula.

Exercise

THIS EXERCISE IS DESIGNED to encourage you to explore the qualities of paint, by working with the most basic of tools – a cardboard spatula, in place of a painting knife. Discover just how well a painting can be created with the minimum of equipment and the maximum of enthusiasm.

Step 1 - The wet thin surface wash accepts bold strokes from the cardboard spatulas. Look for rhythms and general masses, rather than detail.

Step 2 - Apply the first layer of 'knife-work' in strong directional strokes, using heavy pressure. This provides a silhouette into which heavier paint can be built.

Step 3 - For the final step, exploit the qualities of painting wet-into-wet, mixing the colours on the surface and producing that generally flat, yet streaky colour which is so unique to palette knife work. Note how the movement of this streaked paint produces rhythms. Also observe how the background is worked right up to leaf and petal edges, so that colours meet each other solidly, giving them sharp distinction. The white of the flower is first painted a gentle coloured grey ([Yo]+[ro]+[bp]+ [TW]). This is followed by a pure yellow white ([Yo]+[TW]) to suggest sunlight.

COLOUR REFERENCE	COLOUR MIXING
Red-purple [Rp] Red-orange [Ro] Blue-purple [Bp] Blue-green [Bg] Yellow-orange [Yo] Yellow-green [Yg] Underpainting White [UW] Titanium White [TW] Zinc White [ZW]	Where the pre-fix letter is shown in capitals this denotes a larger quantity of that particular colour. Conversely, where the pre-fix letter is shown in a lower case, this denotes a smaller quantity of that particular colour. Example: Bp = **large** amount of blue-purple bp = **small** amount of blue-purple

Stage-by-stage

Before you begin, get a scrap piece of card or board and practice the strokes suggested, without attempting to make them into anything. Simply get the feel of the knife and most importantly, the paint. Study the marks you have made and see what can be learnt from them. How deep are the strokes? How much paint was required? What is the surface like?

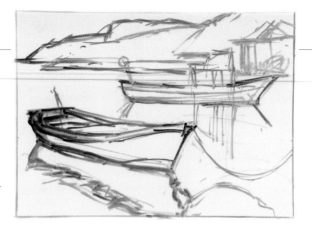

STAGE 1

While palette knife painting involves quite thick layers of paint, the surface nevertheless has a direct effect on the finished stroke. One would imagine that the buttery layers of paint would easily overlay textures. However, any prominence across the surface will lift the knife as it passes over them. Since the knife is stiff, this lift is echoed across the whole width of the stroke, resulting in a line/wall of paint across the stroke. Several prominences and the surface become crisscrossed with these textures. The direction of the stroke will determine the direction in which these surface lines lie and they can be either useful or a nuisance, depending on the desired finish.

It stands to reason that it is far better to start with as smooth a surface as possible, so that knife and paint create their own juicy, unadulterated strokes, without interference from beneath.

A stiff surface is also more resilient to the pressure of paint applied with a knife. As a result, canvas with its inherent texture and give, is not necessarily the ideal surface. Thick paint layers are also more prone to cracking, having dried on a flexible ground.

This project is painted on a thick piece of card, primed with several layers of acrylic gesso primer.

Complete the initial drawing with a brush and thinned colour, for speed and fluidity. In this instance, the border edge, which indicates the frame overlap, is of specific importance. Without it, the negative shape of the sky between frame and hilltop would be impossible to judge.

Since such a large area of the composition is sea, the reflections thereon become a dominant feature. Reflections are created immediately below the subject.

[A] - distant boat seen side-on. This reflection can be easily constructed.

[B] - foreground boat seen at an angle. This requires plotting out. Drop several points to the water's surface and reproduce the measurement beneath to get the general shape of the reflection. Note however, that once the surface becomes disturbed by waves, the reflection, while still lying directly beneath, becomes a little deeper. The more disturbed the surface, the greater the depth of the reflection.

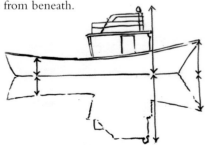

NOTE - in the finished painting - how the reflected image is carried downward/forward on the back slope of the waves. Also that the distant boat has a deeper reflection than the other, since the water in front of it is the most disturbed.

Spread paint as a thin even layer on palette. Wipe blade clean. Scoop up line of colour along blade edge...

...or flex blade gently to pick up colour on tip of blade edge only.

To apply line/thin stroke of colour - run loaded blade edge along surface.

To apply thick stroke of colour - draw loaded blade edge across surface.

STAGE 2

The palette should be cleaned and all traces of thinner removed. You will now be working with colour that comes directly from the tube. To achieve the fluid, succulent stroke that one associates with knife-work painting, it is necessary to work into a wet surface. Such a wet surface pulls the colour from the knife blade.

You could apply a thin layer of one colour across the whole surface to achieve this. In this project a dark underpainting is blocked onto each area, representing the darkest accents of each. Do not worry too much about the quality of the application at this stage, just get the surface covered.

Turn to the headland, where you will see that a start has been made on the second layer of colours in order to demonstrate how the colour beneath provides the accents; while the directional strokes of the painting knife suggest the structure of the landscape.

Once the surface has been covered with paint the colour to be overlaid can be checked by holding the loaded knife in front of it (facing you), before applying it to the wet surface paint.

STAGE 3

As the lights and highlights are applied, the paint on the palette needs to be kept fresh and clean. The mixes will inevitably build and begin to overwhelm the palette. Scoop these mixes up separately and move them to one end of the palette. It would be a pity to waste this paint, so set it to one side for possible future use. Having done this, clean the majority of the palette, in order that fresh paint can be mixed and the painting's vitality maintained.

The painting knife can be used to not only apply paint, but also to remove colour. For line-work or details, such as the window, reverse the blade and use the tip to scrape through the top surface of paint to reveal the under-colour. This technique is known as sgraffito.

By building up a deep mound of colour on the palette, the very point of the knife can be dipped into its centre, to lift up a drip/line of paint from its tip. This is excellent for adding a highlight, or a point of texture.

NOTE - the knife blade needs to be cleaned frequently when used for sgraffito. Otherwise it is likely to re-deposit any paint that has been removed.

Holding the knife horizontally, pull a succession of downward juicy strokes from the boat rail. By starting at the top with the red band, the yellow that follows will effectively sharpen the base line of the red, as it is pulled down from underneath that bottom edge. This works all the way down the boat to the waterline, which provides a sharp edge to the keel, as it too is pulled downward from the base line of the boat.

The brighter reflections on the water are added once the dark underpainting colours have begun to stiffen, as they dry. Whilst the underpainting colours were applied horizontally, the brighter colours are applied vertically. By pulling the knife downwards across the underlying textures, this fresh paint is trapped by the prominence of the previously applied layer - the closest possible scumbling effect that can be produced with a painting knife.

Dark accents are probably more important than the bright colours all around them. Imagine these colours without the darks inside the boat, the dark line along the lower edge of the rail and the dark of the water at the water line. Foreground - if there are not enough darks showing through from the underpainting they need to be added.

Common problems

PROBLEM ONE

Paint applied with a painting knife, by its very nature, tends to be sharply defined along the edges of each stroke. On occasions, when a blended colour is required, this seems impossible, for it would seem that the colour being applied simply overwhelms the paint which is already present on the surface.

PROBLEM TWO

A ground colour cannot be overpainted as it is too powerful, or too deep a layer.

Solution one

Using the edge of the knife, lay the paint in bands of colours, either horizontally, vertically, or more irregularly - do not worry about the colour edges. Clean the painting knife and gently blend the colours together over the surface. Wipe the painting knife frequently, to avoid paint build-up on the blade. Use the flat of the blade for blending, as opposed to the edge.

Just as in brush blending, different results are achieved when moving with, or across, the graduated colours.

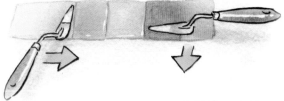

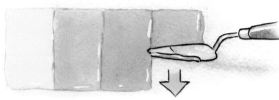

Solution two

Use the knife to scoop or scrape excess colour from the underpainting and lay the fresh colour onto a much more friendly and accepting surface.

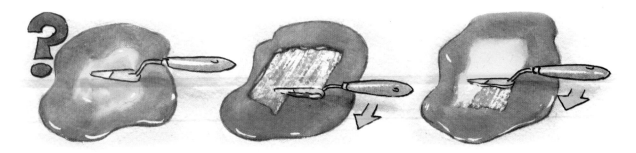

Exploiting brush-strokes

Anyone taking up oil painting for the first time comes face to face with probably the heaviest medium they have ever used. It appears that the paint will never produce soft, gentle strokes, simply because it is so thick and textured.

In spite of these perceived difficulties, the fact is - oil paint does produce qualities which can be as gentle as required. Furthermore, oil paints have the added benefit of being completely within the control of the artist.

The following project will impart one of the most important techniques in oil painting - that of blending. The ability to blend or soften the colour, after it has been applied to the surface, even after a while, is unique to oil painting.

Because the paint remains wet for some time, it can be reworked and adjusted. What at first seems a nuisance becomes one of the all-time benefits of the medium.

WHAT IS SO SPECIAL ABOUT SOFT BRUSH-STROKES?

Firstly, soft brush-strokes help to create volume. Imagine trying to paint a ball with light falling on one side, casting a shadow on the other. The transition from light to dark around its surface, which gives it form, is a smooth one. If all of the brush-strokes remained hard-edged, the ball would seem to have been carved from some rough material. When the brush-strokes blend into one another, the surface becomes smooth.

Now take a more complex form, the human face. Imagine how the brush-strokes need to be soft as they blend into one another and yet retain the various values and hues of the colours applied. So it is we require the ability to blend the internal brush-strokes of an object to suggest its softness or texture.

Look at a photograph of a face or the reflection of yours in a mirror and concentrate on the eyes, which become sharp. The sides of the face curve away from your gaze, toward the ears. The ears, as you keep your focus on the eyes, are a little blurred. For that face to

be painted in sharp silhouette would make it appear flat; instead it needs to be softened or blurred. This requires external blending of the brush-strokes, along the edge of the face and ears. Imagine a full figure, one that is running - painted with sharp edges it would appear frozen in space. To effect the movement in that runner requires both internal and external blending of the legs.

Finally, think of a series of hills, receding into the background. As the hills recede into the distance, they increasingly become lost in the atmospheric mist and so they gradually become more out of focus. Blurring of their silhouette edges is used to create the differing layers of depth that are required to suggest recession.

The ability to blend paint through exploiting brush-strokes will provide you with the tool to create volume, depth and movement. You will be in control of the focus in a painting, allowing you to direct the eye of the viewer. Most importantly, these elements can all be controlled at a leisurely pace, since the paint will not dry out as decisions are being made.

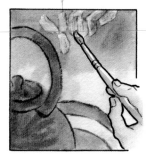

MEDIUM ROUND BRISTLE BRUSH - paint tube colour directly into wet thinner/paint mix.

[SHADOW] apply several values of the same colour - vary directions of stroke.

INTERNAL BLENDING - blend neighbouring colours along their edges using a soft nylon round brush.

Clean brush head frequently by rolling between fingers in absorbent tissue.

EXTERNAL BLENDING - use a small nylon round brush to blend where colours meet. Follow direction of this edge. Keep angle of brush low to surface.

Apply strokes of dark tube colour to teapot using medium round bristle brush.

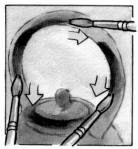

Blend strokes into wet under-painting using a clean bristle brush, cleaning brush head frequently.

Drag, scumble and dab middle value colours onto the wet, dark, stiff layer of tube colour.

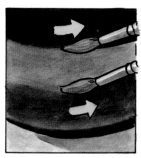

BLEND EDGES by pulling soft nylon round brush along hard edges of paint areas, or...

...STIPPLE by blending hard edges into one another, or...

...SCRATCH into one another (SGRAFFITO blend) - reverse brush and use point of shaft.

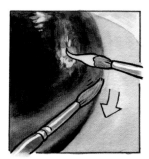

FINAL EXTERNAL BLENDING of some of the silhouette into background. DRIP HIGHLIGHTS onto scuffed middle value impasto texture.

Exercise

This exercise is painted 'Alla Prima' – which simply means that it is painted 'all in one go' and is made up of the first two layers generally associated with an oil painting.

The first layer is produced in paint thinned with turpentine. The composition is drawn in, swiftly followed by the application of fluid thinned colour to eliminate any of the white primed ground.

The second layer is worked with tube consistency paint, laid directly into the previously applied wet, thinned layer. It is built from dark to light, painting wet into wet throughout. To achieve this, the paint must be applied more generously as you move forward toward the highlights.

The choice of brushes can be varied, although it is quite possible to achieve all the work with bristle brushes alone. However, for the first layer, the drawing is more easily accomplished using a nylon Rigger brush, with corrections made using a medium round bristle brush.

The second layer benefits from the use of bristle brushes to build the heavy layers of colour and to dab, daub and scumble the textures.

Blending requires the gentle nature of round nylon brushes to move the paint more slowly. A nylon brush also tends to flatten the textures.

The size of brush employed varies from quite small, for external or edge blending, to larger round brushes, used internally (inside the teapot).

External edges of the object are blended into softness, suggesting lack of focus at this point. The handle seems to blur into depth as a result.

Brush-strokes of both object and background remain unblended and sharp. Our eyes seem to focus in contrast on the softer areas.

Paint strokes inside the object are softened along their edges, producing the soft, rounded effect, of internal blending.

Stage-by-stage

The surface used for this project is a piece of strong card, primed with acrylic gesso primer. This provides a smooth surface on which even the most gentle of impasto layers will be prominent. Since this painting is to be completed without the use of glazes, it is important that every other resource possible is utilised to maximise the inherent texture of the paint. Paint is blocked on swiftly throughout, using bristle brushes – small for the drawing and as large as you can handle for blocking in the colour. The use of a large brush prevents overworking, reminding you that at this stage, painting is simply filling in.

STAGE 1

STEP 1 – Start with the drawing, ensuring that the divisions between background, middle distance and foreground are well marked. Note that not only has the silhouette of the trees been reinforced to separate them from the background, but that the varying depths within the composition are differentiated through the various colours used to produce the drawing.

STEP 2 – This drawing is now swiftly filled in with colour made fluid with thinner. The first colours should be dull, dark versions of the final colour to be applied later. For instance, greens need red added to them to take them toward dark grey green. Similarly, other colours need their matching complementaries added, so that this layer becomes dull, dark and dismal.

NOTE - This is always a difficult stage, but without these dull dark colours, there will be no contrast for the bright, light colours that follow.

Blending is gentler when carried out with a nylon or other soft–haired brush. The angle to the surface needs to be kept as low as practicable. Too steep an angle will tend to encourage the brush to dig too deeply into the paint layer, causing excessive disturbance.

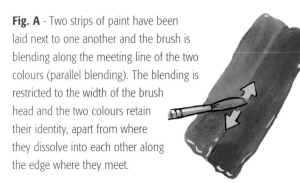

Fig. A - Two strips of paint have been laid next to one another and the brush is blending along the meeting line of the two colours (parallel blending). The blending is restricted to the width of the brush head and the two colours retain their identity, apart from where they dissolve into each other along the edge where they meet.

Fig. B - The blending is slightly diagonal to the meeting line (diagonal blending). The stroke could be made back and forth, but in this case is made in one direction only. As a consequence, the left hand colour moves more into the right during the blending process.

STAGE 2

The brushes and palette should now be cleaned and dried thoroughly, to remove all traces of thinner – which would otherwise hinder the building of layered paint in this stage.

BRISTLE BRUSHES are used throughout, for both application and blending of paint. Generally, the whole of the painting is to be kept soft, but your aim is to graduate the softness. Ensure that bristle brushes used for blending feature brush heads that are really flexible. The bristles should comprise of long filaments that will bend – to smooth paint out, rather than scoop it up. Old brushes that have become worn or stiff should be kept only for mixing paint on the palette.

BACKGROUND – where the light is permeating between large tree trunks. This most distant area serves only as a backdrop to the central subject in this composition – the flowers. Once applied, the tube colour in this area is heavily blended with a large bristle brush.

Fig. C - The blend is more aggressive, since it is made across, or at right angles, to the meeting line of the two colours (right angle blending). Moving between the colours so swiftly, inevitably soils the brush at a faster rate. If the brush is not frequently cleaned it will begin to paint, rather than blend.

Fig. D - In these circumstances the size of brush used does matter. A smaller brush, with its narrower head, will blend the colour more discreetly. However, it will tend to soil more quickly than a larger size and therefore require more frequent cleaning.

MIDDLE DISTANCE AND FOREGROUND

Progressively darker colours must be applied and will serve as accents beneath the lighter values applied over them. These too must be kept soft and unfocussed through blending, but you can switch to smaller bristle brushes for more control. It is useful however to push these dark colours into the surface. There is no benefit in dark colours protruding from the surface, since they are not required to catch the light.

NOTE - This dark wet layer will pull colour from the brush as you overpaint, providing it is not too deep. To successfully layer, there must be more paint on your brush than is lying on the surface.

CLEANING – Cleaning your brushes must not involve the use of turpentine, but should be carried out dry on a clean piece of tissue or cloth. The brush head can be squeezed quite tightly between fingers inside the tissue and rolled until the excessive paint is removed.

NEVER pull at the hairs, as this will dislodge them – resulting in a damaged brush.

STAGE 3

At this stage decisions have to be made as to what will begin to come into focus within the painting. There is still a lot of blending to be done throughout the foliage.

Although the finished painting seems full of detail, look closely at the complex areas of foliage. Emphasis has been placed on rhythms and movements of masses, but there is very little sharpness. Where it does occur, our eyes stop, they gather information and then move on, making us feel that there is more sharp detail than

actually exists. This is the way in which our eyes and brain work, so the situation is accepted as natural.

Take the blue flowers on the left. These are the closest object to the viewer, but they have been softened both internally and externally around their silhouette. Our gaze therefore moves past them to the pink flowers in the centre. These have been blended internally, to suggest their soft form – but their edges have been left sharp. So it is we now identify the 'subject' of this complex composition, as our eyes can easily focus on it.

⇧ **While it may seem strange,** at first, to have something out of focus in the very front of the painting, the possibilities it suggests are enormous. For example, you could frame your subject within a soft foreground. Conversely, you may find that one aspect of a scene is unnecessary. It may not be possible to remove a tree or a building from a view for it to remain recognisable, but there is no reason that all aspects of a composition should draw the viewer's gaze. Instead, leave them out of focus. A large crowd in the foreground could be softened so that one's eyes are drawn over them to a more distant centre of attention.

⇧ **A complex area full of detail?** Look carefully and identify just how much is in focus. Behind the sharp edges of the leaves are soft, dull greens. Without these, the focused areas would simply become lost against a plethora of detail.

⇦ **When we separate an area** such as this from its surroundings, it is possible to see how little information is really carried there. Being so highly blended, it becomes almost an abstract arrangement of soft colours. Yet, without soft areas such as this, the sharp, focused areas of the painting would have nothing against which to contrast. Just as we need to have dark areas to achieve light in a painting, we also need soft areas to effect sharpness. In this way our eyes become excited by the differences of paint quality, as they travel across the surface.

Common problems

PROBLEM

What is so special about oil painting brushes, they seem to be made of the same materials as those used for other media? If you cannot find the right oil painting brush, would a watercolour brush do just as well?

ANSWER

It is quite a reasonable question, for there are watercolour brushes that could be used in oil painting. However, it is important to know when they can and cannot be used so that you can make that decision.

The first thing to recognise is that many oil painting brushes are made from bristle, primarily designed for use with heavy impasto paint. Bristle brushes are quite different from watercolour brushes, which are generally soft and composed of natural hair or nylon.

Softer brushes however are employed in oil painting, for glazing and blending. There is no reason why these should not be watercolour brushes, providing they fulfil certain criteria.

Watercolour Brushes for Oil Painting
The best watercolour brushes are soft and point well. Sadly they are not suitable when it comes to glazing, as the soft brushes might become damaged through being dragged over dry impasto paint. However, watercolour brushes are excellent for blending.

What is the difference between a soft brush for watercolour painting and one for use in oil painting? The main difference is in the length of the handle.

Fig 1. Brushes intended for oil painting feature long handles, so that the painter can be positioned further away from the surface of the painting. In theory, the impasto surface of the oil painting is seen better from further away and is thus painted at a distance.

Fig 2. A long-handled brush is also easier to use overhand, without catching the wet oil painting surface with your hand. This overhand method is an essential brush hold for certain directional strokes.

Fig 3. A long-handled brush allows this grip and still gives you a shallow angle - essential in the application of paint and for the blending technique.

CAUTION: Should you wish to put your soft-haired brushes to use in watercolour painting, it is imperative that they are thoroughly cleaned. Should thinners or oil paint get into watercolours, you will be in serious trouble.

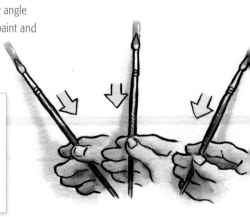

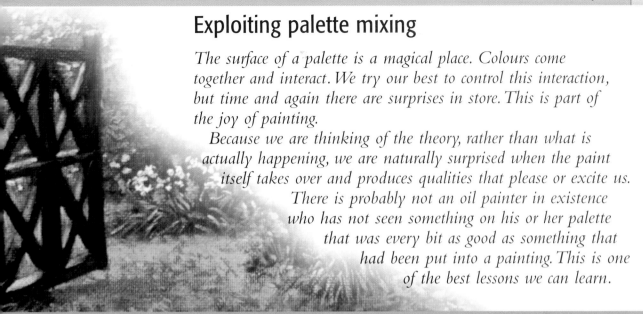

Exploiting palette mixing

The surface of a palette is a magical place. Colours come together and interact. We try our best to control this interaction, but time and again there are surprises in store. This is part of the joy of painting.

Because we are thinking of the theory, rather than what is actually happening, we are naturally surprised when the paint itself takes over and produces qualities that please or excite us. There is probably not an oil painter in existence who has not seen something on his or her palette that was every bit as good as something that had been put into a painting. This is one of the best lessons we can learn.

OIL PAINT IN ITSELF IS EXCITING. There are times when the artist has to listen to what it has to teach them. Going with the flow is a wonderful experience, but it takes a lot of confidence to let the paint speak for you. The first squeeze of an oil paint tube introduces heavy looking paint to the palette surface. This is your base material. What you now require is the knowledge that will enable you to mix it with other colours and, just as importantly, to change its nature through the addition of thinners and mediums.

This will at first seem terribly confusing and may well prompt the question, why can't the paint be used in its natural state?

In the following exercise and project you will learn exactly why thinners and mediums are used, what happens when they are mixed with paint, how to use them and which to choose to serve a particular purpose.

It is only when armed with this knowledge that you can make an informed choice as to which technique in oil painting suits you best. Through the use of thinners and mediums a far greater choice is at your disposal. The physical nature of paint also changes as you add them. From a practical point of view you need to be in control of the quantities of each as they mix

on the palette. Not only is it necessary to keep them from running all over the place, it is essential to avoid mixing vast quantities of unwanted paint.

It is important to understand at which point this range of mixing processes should take place during the various stages of the painting process. Were this to be ignored, the stability of your finished painting could be put at risk.

You need to take on board the fact that oil painting is about working from lean to fat (the nature of the paint) and from thick to thin (the nature of the layers). This means that the paint must progressively have more oil in its mix, as the layers are built up one on top of another.

Furthermore, a controlled method is required for adding both colours and mediums to your paint mixes that will become second nature. This is essential in freeing up your time to concentrate on the painting at hand, rather than worrying about your paint mixes and materials.

This is what palette mixing is all about and by following the principles demonstrated on the pages that follow you will not only gain insight into the full range of palette mixes available, you will also benefit from a finished painting that is stable and will stand the test of time.

UNDERPAINTING - Palette mixes are fluid with thinner. Loose mixtures with which to draw and cover the surface swiftly.

Apply thinned colour with bristle brushes. Note warm colours in background to provide contrast for cools shadows to follow.

IMPASTO LAYER - Clean palette to remove thinner. Make stiff, tube consistency mixes. Use underpainting white (dries swiftly and produces stable impasto surface).

Stiff paint builds up deep textures. Keep palette mixes light so that they take glazes to follow, without becoming too dark.

TINTS - Introduce zinc white (transparent) to palette and gradually draw small quantity of blue into its edge until correct mix is achieved.

Introduce a fluid glazing medium (alkyd). Merge gently into the edge of the stiff mix until the correct density of tint is reached.

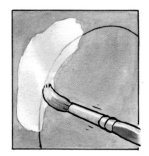

To apply tints use a soft-headed brush. This brush helps to blend tints over silhouette edges to soften them...

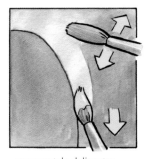

...or accurately delineates edges to make them sharper [bottom]. These can be blended into the background instead, forcing it to recede [top].

GLAZES - Several viscosities of glazing medium exist and/or you can also add a small amount of thinner to the glaze mix on the palette.

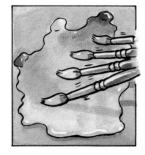

Glazing mixes can be made of a single colour, or several. Paint should be placed at edge of medium to facilitate rapid colour range.

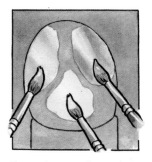

Glaze colours can be used to cover large areas thinly - with a medium to large soft brush, or...

...be used fluidly with a fine brush (or Rigger brush) for drawing and detail.

Exercise

Since this exercise encompasses the complete principle of painting in oils, it is sensible to pick a simple subject with which to experiment. As with any still-life arrangement, you need to consider how the light source affects the composition. Side light is perfect, but if you rely on sunlight, remember that it moves. If you prefer to work from life, it is probably better to set up an artificial light source.

Complete the drawing and underpainting layers with lean paint. Add thinner to the mix on the palette – this makes it fluid, not only for swift application, but also to spread out both the oil and pigment in the mix. Do not over worry about palette mixes at this stage; as long as they are kept dark they will form an excellent underpainting.

Use a small bristle brush and the thinnest colour to draw in the simple shapes of egg and egg cup. Block in overall with warm colours and redraw where necessary. Remove all traces of thinner from your brush and palette before moving on to the stiff, impasto mixes to follow.

The stiff paint mixes that you are now to use to build toward light require Underpainting white, which creates a viscous mix, quite unlike other painting whites, such as Titanium white. Be generous with the amount mixed on the palette and loaded onto the brush, to allow you to create impasto qualities that will suppress the regular weave of the canvas texture. Keep the colour mixes as streaky as possible on the palette. In other words, do not over-mix or you could ruin the quality of the paint strokes.

Using bristle brushes to apply and blend paint, build up the values from dark to light across the painting. Blending is not only important to create the rounded volume of egg and cup, but also to keep the shadow edges soft. Allow this alla prima stage to dry thoroughly before moving onto tinting and glazing.

TINTS - Use soft nylon brushes. Apply behind the egg to add depth and selectively soften its silhouette. Note that on the left hand side of the shell the tint overlaps the edge and so it dissolves into depth. Down the right hand side, the tint actually sharpens the shell edges, with the application of a fluid, sharp edged tint.

During the palette mixing of tints, it is sensible to use a bristle brush, so that again the paint is not over-mixed. Whereas, blending of both tints and glazes is done with soft brushes, working them into the dry, underlying textures.

GLAZES AND FINAL ACCENTS - Use a soft round brush and Rigger brush to restore any of the colours and contrast lost during the tinting stage.

FINALLY - Use a tube consistency warm white (Titanium white [TW] + [yo]) to scuff colour in front of the egg cup, behind its right hand edge and on some speckles on the eggshell, to add a touch of sparkle to the finished piece.

NOTE - THE EGG IS SLIGHTLY OFF TRUE. HOLD YOUR BRUSH VERTICALLY IN FRONT OF THE IMAGE TO SEE THAT IT LEANS GENTLY TO THE LEFT. THIS SORT OF IRREGULARITY ADDS CHARACTER TO ANY STUDY.

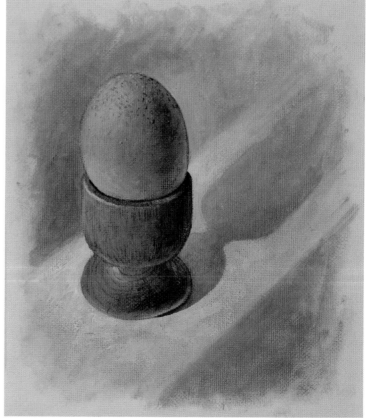

Stage-by-stage

This painting could really be called a study in greens, for it features every colour nuance from dark to light and cool to warm. So dominant is the colour that you will need to call on every element of palette mixing at your disposal. This project will help you to discover the full potential of mixing the paint into differing consistencies for the various layers of colour that are to be employed.

STAGE 1

STEP 1 - Draw the outline of the various elements within the composition.

STEP 2 - Now complete the first layer of thinned colour, by filling in the various areas with colours that are complementary to those in the final painting. For example, an area that is to be finished in yellow green should be painted at this stage in purple red.

While most of this first layer will be covered by subsequent painting, any tiny areas that do remain will provide that extra kick of contrast which this very green painting requires.

Firstly, mix the colours dry on the palette surface. As solid colour they are far easier to see and to control. Gradually add turpentine substitute to the edge of the mix little by little. In this way you will not end up with large paint flows dripping from your palette and the colour mix can be easily changed as you go along.

NOTE - TURPENTINE DILUTED COLOUR GOES A LONG WAY AND YOU ONLY NEED A THIN LAYER, SO IT IS A WASTE OF PAINT TO MIX VAST QUANTITIES.

In this example the basic colour (yellow) is developed in several different directions, before the thinner is introduced from the side. This not only saves paint, but it also saves space on your palette. At the beginning of a painting, it is often useful for the colours to be of the same family. This unifies the colour balance to some extent, allowing you to concentrate on value (light to dark) changes. The latter are far more important in achieving a sense of light and depth. Starting with too many colours on the painting surface can be a distraction. Always remember that this first layer of colour is only the underpainting. Its most important job is to cover the white of the surface, so that from this point on you will be painting colour on colour. The colours cannot be seen properly until all the white is removed. It makes sense not to worry overmuch about the colours being applied, until all the white disappears.

STAGE 2

From this point on the turpentine is entirely eliminated from the palette surface. Brushes can be cleaned in turpentine between colours, but must be carefully dried on tissue or cloth before being brought back into action.

The paint is used at tube consistency, exploiting its stiff impasto qualities. Note the variety of strokes employed. Even simple areas such as the sky are not entirely overpainted. There is variety in the direction of the strokes and the surface coverage is irregular. As a result we can see down through the layers of colour and this excites the eye.

The general rule is, the darker the colour, the less texture it need have. Bright highlight colours, on the other hand, protrude from the surface and in so doing, catch ambient light.

On the palette - start with dark mixes first, gradually adding lighter colour and/or white from the sides, as before, so that the mix is always under control. Make sure that the paint mixes begin generously. You cannot build impasto layers of colour without plenty of paint. If you do not start with enough colour on your palette, you could run out before the layers have been built up. This will prove frustrating as you try to accurately replicate the same colours.

Even worse, you could resort to making do with a sparsely loaded brush. However, it is impossible to paint wet-on-wet unless you progressively load the brush with increasingly generous amounts of paint.

Eventually, you will find this one of the most rewarding aspects of painting with oils, as you wield fluid succulent paint across the painting surface.

Fig. A - Many artists believe that it is bad practice to mix colour with a brush. There is no doubt that this can cause wear to the brush and damage is much more likely if a soft brush (nylon or sable) is employed. A bristle brush however, being a little tougher, can do the job excellently. If in doubt, use a larger brush and/or a cheaper variety than that with which you are to apply the paint.

Fig. B- The advantage of brush mixing is that it is often incomplete, provided the mix is not overworked. In other words, the paint mix remains slightly streaky, even as it is applied to the painting. This makes for a much more exciting paint stroke than colour mixed with a palette knife. The knife does the job too well, resulting in a mix that is flat in nature. The pressure employed in knife mixing also seems to take the life out of the paint particles. Even when palette knife painting, try not to over-mix or over-work the paint on the palette surface.

⇧ **Depth is achieved over a relatively small area,** through the careful manipulation of aerial perspective. Note how the green becomes both warmer and darker towards the front of the painting. Equally important is the warm colour between the green strokes. These accents are heavier, warmer and darker as they move forward. They also provide a complementary contrast to the greens, making them brighter.

⇧ **Distant trees, stone wall and bush are all impasto layers,** built wet-on-wet. You can easily see how the lighter values have the most texture. Overlaid glazes run into these brush-strokes, further enhancing their texture. Final lights and highlights, scuffed over these glazes, catch the impasto high points and really seem to glint by contrast.

STAGE 3

Such a busy painting, such a lot of depth to capture. The simple answer is to work with tints. On the palette produce a dry mix of blue and zinc white, with a fluid alkyd medium added from the side. This tint can be more or less opaque, depending on the amount of white in the mix.

In this painting the tint is firstly used to push the sky and mountain back from the ridge of the roof. Then it is used to bring the wall forward from the building and helps give depth to the grassed area.

Glazes – similarly fluid mixes, without white added, to make them transparent. The resultant glazes are used to add richness and texture. Here they are used to add character to the wall and building, as well as across the various greens (imbuing them with greater variety of hue and luminosity).

These mixes are difficult to judge while on the palette surface and should be tested on tiny spots on the surface, before being committed to larger areas.

NOTE - PALETTE SURFACES MUST BE KEPT PRISTINE FOR GLAZES AND TINTS, SO THAT THEY ARE NOT POLLUTED BY EARLIER MIXES, ESPECIALLY THOSE THAT WERE OPAQUE.

⇧ **Blue tints, applied all around the standing stone** at the end of the wall, push it forward in space, against the bush and building behind. Once you have identified the tint, note how it is stronger toward the stone. As it moves away from the stonework, the blue tint is diminished by blending and it is impossible to determine where it actually disappears. Instead, our eyes pick out the point of greatest change (at the stone edge) and we perceive the contrast that is required to suggest depth. Identify the other edges within the painting where this occurs - gate, hedge, mountains and sky.

Common problems

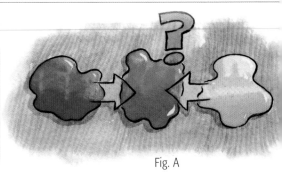

Fig. A

REASON

Some colours possess a greater staining power than others. This is known as their tinting strength and has nothing to do with the theory of colour mixing. Put simply, some colours are stronger than others and can easily overpower mixes.

Fig. B - To achieve a middle orange in this case requires that much less red be used.

Fig. B

NOTE - PRUSSIAN BLUE [BG] ALSO HAS A VERY POWERFUL TINTING STRENGTH AND VERY LITTLE IS REQUIRED WHEN MIXING GREEN.

In time, experience will teach you which colours are the most powerful in mixes. However, no matter how experienced you become, some colours, such as Prussian Blue, will always catch you by surprise - unless you employ a method by which you can control these mixes.

SOLUTION

Fig. C - The simple answer is, never add strong colours directly to a mix.

Fig. C

Fig. D

Fig D. Transfer some onto another part of your palette. Remove most of the colour from the brush by rotating it on the surface of the palette. Only now take the brush to the mix. If more is needed, return to your clean deposit and repeat the process, until the colour mix is what you require. This prevents you from not only becoming frustrated, but from wasting costly paint.

Discovering surface texture

Layers and surfaces are the very foundation of oil painting. The colour itself is delivered within the tube as a stiff thick paint. This naturally creates impasto, or textured, brush-strokes and this ability to create textures cannot be ignored, if you are to fully exploit the potential inherent in painting with oils.

The surface therefore needs to be as strong as the paint itself. Heavy paint requires a ground to which it can adhere and one that will not cause the dried paint to crack and subsequently fall away.

TRADITIONALLY, THE BASE FOR OIL PAINTING IS CANVAS, although almost any surface that is reasonably rigid will suffice, as long as it is properly prepared. All base surfaces feature an inherent texture, which can either be incorporated into the composition, or obliterated by the paints texture.

While the thought of obliterating the surface texture by over-painting another may sound negative, it does in fact have positive benefits. Heavy texture underlying the painting demands the application of heavy, structured over-painting. This forces the painter to make full use of juicy and vigorous brush-strokes.

However the ground is simply the base layer at which the process begins. Once paint is applied, the true nature of the oil painting surface demands our attention. Paint applied over paint begins to build a weave of structure across the surface. Since the oil dries as it reacts with the air, there is no evaporation and therefore the volume of the paint remains unaffected. Whatever has been built on the surface will remain intact and when dry, will last for several lifetimes.

These textures are never fully visible until they are glazed. If you have ever been enthralled by the fluid juiciness of an Old Master's brush-strokes, it is probably because the painting was well glazed, enabling the viewer to see them easily.

The wonderful property of oil glazes is that they also remain stable as they dry. They neither lighten, nor fade away, but remain as delicious as when they were initially laid down. Glazes should not be readily identifiable in the finished painting. Their purpose is to expose and thus enhance the impasto textures over which they are painted.

Where to start and how much texture and glaze should be used? Can these techniques be overdone and, if so, how can they be restored?

It is only through experimenting with textures and glazes that their potential can be fully understood. The following project starts by exploring textures, explaining the differences between arbitrary texture and structural texture and what each can bring to the repertoire of techniques at your disposal.

We then move on to glazing and how this technique affects the surface texture and exactly what the application of glazes does to the values and hues of applied colours. This also includes the technique of tinting, where glazes are made semi-opaque.

The stage-by-stage painting demonstrates how colour mixing can be created in transparent and semi-transparent layers.

It is essential that the surface is exploited to its fullest, for in so doing you will find surprises that will excite you and qualities that will make those looking at your paintings wonder how you created them. Be patient and keep your mind open to the possibilities for there is something for everyone when they master the surfaces of oil painting.

ARBITRARY TEXTURE - is laid over the primed surface. Oil whites take time to dry. Instead use acrylic modelling paste. Vary direction of brush-strokes.

UNDERPAINTING - Once dry, complete drawing and fill in with thinned washes of oil colour. Redraw with nylon Rigger brush.

Once this layer is dry, switch to stiff tube colour and scrub in some darker underpainting.

IMPASTO - Use Underpainting white to create generous streaky mixes of colour on the palette.

Scuff these over the surface, keeping the brush low to make the most of arbitrary texture beneath.

STRUCTURAL TEXTURE - Create generous mix of colour. Colour of mix is less important than keeping it light.

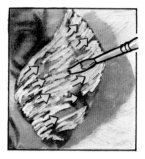

Draw these strokes around the form as if you were carving them from space.

With smaller bristle brush - dip into deep mix on palette and sharply withdraw, to create a point of paint.

Use this technique to drip impasto highlights onto prominent details on surface of shell.

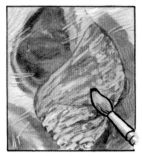

Allow work to dry. Glaze with very fluid glazing medium - which runs into surface textures. Two thin layers are better than one thick layer.

Strokes or daubs of fluid glaze can be made into this surface while still wet.

Final points of accent or line-work are produced with a small fine or Rigger brush. Use just a little glazing medium to keep fluid.

Exercise

Although transparent glazes are a natural feature to exploit in oil painting, they are not valid until there is a sufficiently textured surface on which they can work effectively. Two forms of surface texture can be applied – arbitrary and structural.

In this exercise, arbitrary texture is created to form the first painting surface, through the introduction of acrylic texture paste (modelling paste). Acrylic makes a perfect medium for this technique, as it is strong and bonds well with the oil that is applied over it. Whilst there is nothing wrong with using an oil paint to produce this textured surface, it does take longer to dry.

Arbitrary texture breaks up overlaid colours in an irregular fashion. It makes the surface more exciting to the eye. Being quite powerful, it will force you to be bold with overlaid structural texture.

The second layer of texture follows the forms and structures of the subject. It is very sculptural and especially effective when painting a subject whose inherent texture is an important aspect of its form.

Both textures will become more visible with the application of glazes. In this case, an oily thinner was used as the medium in the glaze mix. Oily thinner can be made of fifty percent turpentine substitute and fifty percent linseed oil. The linseed oil in the mix takes a while to dry, which allows for plenty of time to make adjustments, should you wish to partially or totally remove any of the glazes.

COLOUR REFERENCE

Red-purple	[Rp]
Red-orange	[Ro]
Blue-purple	[Bp]
Blue-green	[Bg]
Yellow-orange	[Yo]
Yellow-green	[Yg]

Underpainting White [UW]
Titanium White [TW]
Zinc White [ZW]

COLOUR MIXING
Where the pre-fix letter is shown in capitals this denotes a larger quantity of that particular colour.

Conversely, where the pre-fix letter is shown in a lower case, this denotes a smaller quantity of that particular colour.

Example:
Bp = **large** amount of blue-purple
bp = **small** amount of blue-purple

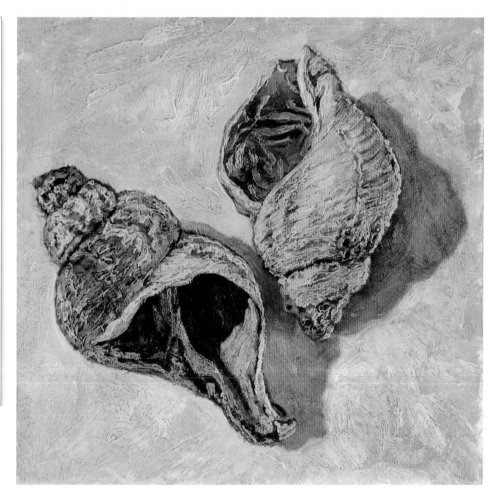

Stage-by-stage

STAGE 1

While it is usual for the impasto surface to develop during the middle process of a painting, this project begins with it instead. This initial textured surface will affect and control all of the paint layers that follow. In effect, it forms a textural underpainting into which you will be running fluid colours.

The first step is to apply arbitrary texture on the primed ground. An example of arbitrary texture is to be found in the earliest work known; that of cave paintings; in which the artist exploited the irregular (arbitrary) textures of the cave walls so that they became an intrinsic part of the finished work.

The arbitrary texture in this painting is created with paint. Use a bristle brush to generously cover the ground with underpainting white and ensure that your strokes travel in all directions to excite the surface. To speed up drying time, this first layer could be executed using either acrylic texture paste, or white acrylic paint.

Once this surface is dry, complete the drawing, using a fine nylon brush or Rigger. Block in the composition masses with gentle colour mixed with generous amounts of thinner. These transparent washes separate the areas and bring out the texture.

The second step is to produce a surface comprising of structural texture. Structural texture is composed of brush-strokes that follow the rhythm of the subject. Were you painting a ball, the strokes would move around its contours, as if you were modelling the ball over the surface. On the other hand, a tree might have radiating strokes to suggest its fine branches.

Structural strokes therefore relate directly to the objects and shapes within the composition. Again, paint these with a bristle brush loaded with Underpainting white. On this occasion however, add a little colour to the mix so that the forms and shapes can be separately identified.

NOTE - DO NOT USE ACRYLIC AFTER THIS POINT, AS YOU NOW HAVE A THIN LAYER OF OIL ON THE SURFACE.

FIRST THREE STEPS IN STAGE ONE

Fig. 1 - Cover prepared ground with a layer of arbitrary texture. This can be oil (Underpainting white) or acrylic (texture paste). Apply with a large round bristle brush to ensure surface brush-strokes are highly visible and brush in all directions.

Fig. 2 - Once arbitrary texture has dried, use medium soft brush to flood thinned grey colours on to depict masses. Use smaller soft round brush to carry out line-work.

Fig. 3 - Once this has dried apply structural texture, using a medium bristle brush and a paint mix comprising Underpainting white with a hint of colour added, to make it easier to see. Leave to dry thoroughly before proceeding to the next stage.

STAGE 2

Prepare glazes on the palette using either an oily thinner, or a fluid alkyd medium, thinned with a little turpentine substitute.

As these glazes begin to flow across the painting surface, you will really start to see the nature of the texture beneath. The purpose of this stage is that you be as creative as possible developing these textures as they are revealed.

Note the most transparent glazes, which are to be found on the mountain [Bp+ro+yo], the foreground snow [Bg+ro] and the tree bark in the foreground [Bg+ro+yg]. Whilst these produce the dark values of the painting, they are lighter (more medium added) into the distance to suggest aerial perspective.

To achieve extra contrast, wipe surfaces with a thumb or finger to remove some glaze from the most protruding textures.

Add Zinc white to some glazed areas to turn them into semi-opaque tints. For example, the lake [Bp+ro+ZW], the far distant mountain [Bp+ro+yg+ZW] and the distant snow [Bp+ro+ZW].

Use darker concentrations of glaze [Bg+ro+yo] to draw in line-work and detail into the wet surface. Examples of this are to be found in the fine branches of the foreground and the distant trees. It is also apparent in the distant textures of the mountain, where it is interwoven with the textural qualities already exhibited by the glazes. Use a fine pointed nylon brush or Rigger to drag and pull the line across the irregularities in a visually exciting manner.

FINGER WIPING - A finger or thumb wiped across the surface of a glaze, with considerable pressure, lifts or smears the fluid surface. Depending on the depth of the dry texture beneath, the technique tends to lift more glaze from the highest points of the impasto and leaves it in the valleys.

FINGER TONKING - On the other hand, the gentler technique of finger tonking can be used to reduce paint strokes. This is a dabbing motion, where the finger is pressed against the wet paint and on lifting removes a little colour with it. The amount of lift depends on both the fluidity of the colour and the pressure exerted. Still wet, fluid line-work for example, can be reduced or removed effectively with this technique (tree branches).

⇦ **The mountain probably carries** the bulk of the transparent glazed texture within the painting. Note that while the directions of these textures suggest the structure of rock and tree, the values of the colours are all very close. Half close your eyes and you will see how all of the colours meld into a solid mass, which is the perfect foil for the brightness of the sky and water.

⇦ **Glazes run into the structural textures** of the paint and suggest all of the fine branches that would look far too dominant if painted more meticulously. The scuffs of more solid paint used across the water intrude into the tree's shape, making it feel more open and improving its silhouette.

STAGE 3

Opaque scuffs and strokes are now employed throughout the painting. In the graduated colour mixes for the sky and mountains this involves adding both white for opacity (Titanium white) and medium for fluidity (alkyd). Working across the sky, paint the spaces between the branches to tighten up their structures (negative painting).

Scuff the colour mix [Bg+Ro+TW] over the cliffs to provide texture, using the flattened shoulder of a soft round brush. The point of the brush can be used for detail, such as working right up to edges, or into the crevices of the surface texture.

The water, wall and snow on the ground are all painted with tube consistency paint to achieve the density needed for the heavy snow layers – shadow [Bp+ro+yo+TW], sunlight [Yo+yg+TW].

However, medium needs to be added to the colour mix for the tree branches, where the colour is applied in many areas with a Rigger, dragged level with the surface, to create fluid scuffs across the rough texture.

Highlights are dripped on with tube consistency colour for that final impasto touch [TW+yg], which will effectively capture the light and add a sparkle.

⇩ **One of the most defined and dramatic textures** of the painting is that embodied in the stone wall. Dark under-painting rubbed into the impasto strokes is followed by scuffs of medium blue. In most cases a wall across the front of a composition would act as a barrier within the painting. In this painting however, the wall is so eclipsed by its own texture that it dissolves into the painting.

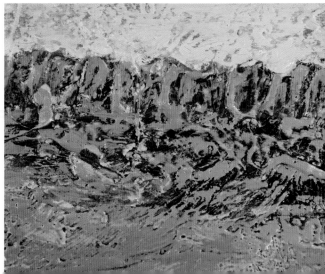

Common problems

PROBLEM

Many painters have trouble with glazes, when using them for the first time. Glazing is an exciting technique, but this can lead to over exuberance in its use. While glazes should enhance impasto textures, they can, on occasions, become too heavy and too dark.

By using glazes judiciously you can have recourse to thirty or more glaze layers in your painting. Imagine what would happen were these to be applied too strongly!

SOLUTION

The success of a glaze depends on two factors.

First, the impasto nature of the surface to be glazed. The deeper the textures, the more glazes they can take.

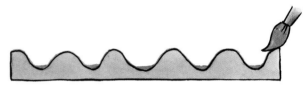

Fig. 1

Second, the fluidity of the glazing medium will affect the quality of the result.

These two aspects must be in balance for your glaze to work. Remember, whatever texture you have created will be exaggerated by the glaze.

Fig. 2

Fig. 1 Use a fluid medium in your glaze colour and it will run into the depths of the texture very easily.

Fig. 2 Should the glazing medium be a little stiffer, the layer will stay a little thicker on the raised point and be heavier in the furrows.

Fig. 3 Impasto gel glazing medium may be sufficiently viscous to apply with a palette knife and can entomb the impasto layer in transparent, or semi-transparent colour.

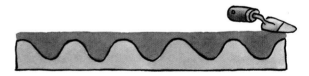

Fig. 3

Fig. 4 Although it is possible to remove the top layer of all glazes, bear in mind that it is the most fluid, which allow you the most opportunity for the application of further thin glaze layers of differing colours.

Fig. 4

Useful information

PAINTING KIT NEEDED TO COMPLETE THE TUTORIALS IN THIS BOOK

Oil Tube Paints (Pages 14 & 15)
Red-orange (Cadmium Red Deep)
Red-purple (Alizarin Crimson)
Yellow-green (Lemon or Primary Yellow)
Yellow-orange (Cadmium Yellow Deep)
Blue-green (Prussian Blue)
Blue-purple (Ultramarine)
Titanium White (TW)
Zinc White (ZW)
Underpainting White (UW)

Oil Brushes (Long Handled) (Pages 22 & 23)
Round Bristle Oil Brush
Soft Round Nylon Oil Brush
Flat Bristle Oil Brush
Large Nylon Rigger Brush

Oil Palette (Pages 30 & 31)
Wooden Oval (Medium)

Artists' Distilled Turpentine
Alkyd Medium
Acrylic Gesso Primer
Canvas Boards or Oil Paper
Painting Knife
Palette Knife
Retouching Varnish

OCCASIONAL GLOSSARY

TERMS
Aerial Perspective
A sense of distance, usually within a landscape, caused by diminishing colour values and colour temperature.

Colour Temperature
The suggestion of warmth or coolness conveyed to varying degrees by all colours.

Negative Painting
Painting the space around an object, rather than the object itself.

Density of Colour
The measure of pigment carried within any paint.

Consistency of Paint
The degree of fluidity or solidity of paint, in its raw form or in mixes.

REFERENCES
Colour Reference
Red-purple [Rp]
Red-orange [Ro]
Blue-purple [Bp]
Blue-green [Bg]
Yellow-orange [Yo]
Yellow-green [Yg]

Underpainting White [UW]
Titanium White [TW]
Zinc White [ZW]

COLOUR MIXING
Where the pre-fix letter is shown in capitals this denotes a larger quantity of that particular colour. Conversely, where the pre-fix letter is shown in a lower case, this denotes a smaller quantity of that particular colour.

E.G.
Bp = large amount of blue-purple
bp = small amount of blue-purple

Hue, Value, Tone
Hue is a bright primary or secondary colour on the basic colour circle.

Value is the degree of lightness or darkness of a colour.

Tone is the degree of lightness or darkness of a neutral grey.

Lights
The lightest hue of colour in any particular section of a painted area.

Highlights
The tiny point of light on the surface at which the light source is reflected. This reflected light maybe white, or a colour.

Accents
The darkest points of shadow of an object.

ART WORKSHOP WITH PAUL
Tuition and Guidance for the Artist in Everyone ◗

Log on to the artworkshopwithpaul.com website for downloadable tutorials and Art Clinic, relating to working with watercolours, oils, acrylics, pastels, drawing and other media.

Check out Paul's Bookshelf for details of all his books. Visit **Paul's Gallery** and the various galleries showing original paintings, limited edition prints, commissioned work, examples of collected works and work in progress.

Catch up on the latest news and details of Art Workshop With Paul Taggart Painting Breaks & Courses.

Alternatively you can write to
Art Workshop With Paul Taggart / FS
c/o Promark, Studio 282, 24 Station Square, Inverness, Scotland, IV1 1LD

Or email
mail@artworkshopwithpaul.com

Artstrips©
Fully narrated and detailed step-by-step demonstrations form the basis of all Paul Taggart's live tutorials.

To translate these into publishable form was his ambition and thus it was that twenty years ago he conceived of the Artstrips©.

Unique to Paul Taggart, these Artstrips© are intended as a universally understood method of visually conveying detailed instructions.

Paul Taggart

Fine Artist & Author Paul Taggart

From his home in the Northern Highlands of Scotland, professional Fine Artist & Author Paul Taggart shares his enthusiasm for painting with a global audience, through the many books he has written and his extensive website. Paul Taggart's passion for art started at a very early age and ever since gaining a degree in Fine Art over thirty years ago has enjoyed the patronage of collectors, who have purchased an extensive collection of original paintings and limited edition prints.

In line with his belief that everyone should be encouraged to express themselves creatively, Paul Taggart considers it a privilege to have been able to work with aspiring artists throughout that period and to continue to do so. His aim is to provide the right sort of practical help and encouragement in a 'no-nonsense' style that makes the pursuit of painting and drawing accessible to all.

His extensive knowledge across all media in these fields proves invaluable to those following his tutorials, whether through books, the website or when attending his painting breaks and workshops.

Watercolours, oils, acrylics, pastels, drawing and mixed media – all can be developed through Paul Taggart's thorough method of tutoring, honed over many decades of listening to aspiring artists and understanding what they need to achieve their pursuit.

Art Workshop With Paul Taggart is the banner under which Paul Taggart offers a variety of learning aids, projects and events, which include books, videos, internet tutorials, painting breaks and courses.

ACKNOWLEDGEMENTS

Key people have played a major role in my life and in whom I place my unreserved trust - to them, as always, I say a heartfelt thank you. Eileen (my Life & Business Partner) and I, are delighted to dedicate this series of books to someone who has brought them to life, who wholeheartedly joined us in our work some while ago and now gets to see the fruits of her labours – Sunita Gahir. Since setting the design style for my previous series of six books, she has become an invaluable friend, both privately and professionally.

My professional life is split into painting a body of collectable originals, fulfilling commissions, producing material for books and my website, as well as tutoring aspiring painters in painting breaks etc. It is only through the continued patronage of collectors and demand for tutoring from painters that my life as a Professional Fine Artist can continue. Not forgetting those publishers with whom I share a mutual professional trust – most particularly Robert and Susan Guy of Sandcastle Books, who got this series off to a flying start.

Paul Taggart